THE VIEW FROM RIGHT FIELD

THE VIEW FROM RIGHT FIELD

Michele Moore Veldhoen

Michele Moore Veldhoen Publishing

©2018 Michele Moore Veldhoen

All rights reserved. No part of this book may be reproduced or transmitted in any form or by any means—graphic, electronic or mechanical—without the prior written permission of the publisher, except by a reviewer who may quote brief passages in a review.

ISBN: 978-1-7753420-0-7 (paper) - 978-1-7753420-1-4 (EPUB)

The stories in this book adhere as closely to fact as the author's memory is capable. In some cases, events may be compressed, or repositioned for the purposes of narrative convenience. The dialogue in this book is representative of conversations the author remembers and has retold to portray events the author experienced, and are not meant to be viewed as word-for-word transcripts. All characters in this book are real and have given permission to use their names, except in the case of one player and one other person, whose names have been changed to protect privacy.

Cover and interior design by Human Powered Design

Cover photo Cheryl Holt - pexels.com

A special thanks to Eagle Business Coaching and Verdolin Solutions Inc. for their invaluable financial, professional, and personal support in the creation of this book.

Published by Michele Moore Veldhoen Publishing
Calgary, AB Canada
thetreeswallow.com

Printed in Canada by Friesens Press

*Dedicated to
the Okotoks Rainbows Ladies Slo-Pitch Team
1981-2001.*

*May we all get to make a few more plays
before the game is over.*

ACKNOWLEDGEMENTS

I FIRST MET MY EDITOR, AUTHOR BETTY JANE HEGERAT, IN 2009, when she was the Writer-in-Residence at the Calgary Memorial Library. I had followed the advice of a writer friend and sent a sample of my first novel to Betty Jane for feedback. Nervous as a colt in its first thunderstorm, I entered the lamp lit, cubby hole of a room in which Betty Jane received shaky aspiring authors like me. The first thing she said as we sat down together was, 'you know you're a writer, don't you?'

There is not room enough here to convey in words the profound influence Betty Jane's words had on me. Those words have driven me to continue on the long and lonely writing path. I thank Betty Jane, for her words, and her constant support and work on this and all my projects.

Ana Maria Ortega of Eagle Business Coaching is a feisty, smart business and marketing strategist and friend who, when I described this project to her, decided I could, should, and would, become an indie author. Ana Maria set up my first web page and with her irresistible smile and firm hand coaxed me onto social media platforms and other useful online tools, taught me how to use them, and kept me on schedule as we worked together toward the realization of this project. She also fed me delicious food during our working sessions, special dishes of her home country of Ecuador. I cannot imagine how I would have completed this leg of the journey without her. I offer my gratitude to Ana Maria.

I also cannot imagine how I would have converted the vision of this book into reality without the moral and practical support of Debbie Miller, our de facto Rainbows boss. From the moment I first pitched the idea of a memoir, Debbie told me to 'go for it', and had my back, watching for any misses I might make in the story, and catching mistakes before they hit the printer. Most important, she helped me believe the project was worthwhile and it should be launched the way the Rainbows did everything, with irreverence and style. Herding our team to league games, tournaments, and national tours, and later, helping me toward the launch of this memoir, have been Debbie's signature plays. Many, many thanks, to Ms. Debbie Miller.

There are family and friends in my life. Family and friends that I feel watching out for me, cheering me on. When thinking of them now, I feel so fortunate. I am deeply grateful for them, and thank each of them for their encouragement, support, and understanding.

SLO-PITCH: A VARIATION OF THE GAME OF SOFTBALL, IN WHICH an over-sized ball is pitched to the batter in a slow high arc, allowing players with marginal skills a chance at hitting it. Thus, the name slo-pitch. Other unique features include an additional fielder, known as a rover. Rover is not a dog, she's a real live human player. Another notable variation is the prohibition of base stealing. Due to these modifications to the traditional game of softball, slo-pitch is a highly accessible sport for the average recreational athlete or restless sloth.

The Rainbows, Okotoks, Alberta, 1985, Author is first player on left, bottom row (wearing shirt with rainbow)

INTRODUCTION

Along with a hot Mediterranean looking boy named Scott Decembrini and my collection of Nancy Drew mysteries, when I was a little girl, playing ball was a love of my life. On game days I was delirious with excitement, anticipation, and joy. I was the team shortstop, and was sure I was the best shortstop in the girls' softball world. This may have had something to do with my sense of life satisfaction.

There's status associated with the position of shortstop. Status and glory: the equivalent of being the lead singer in a band, the bull rider in the local rodeo, or the drummer on a dragon boat team. And to really elevate my perception, I was Princess in a Royal Family. The Queen, like a pitcher, may be the boss, but we all know the Princess gets all the attention and has all the fun.

At the sight or sound of the word 'shortstop' my brain floods with prized memories. Standing in my zone between second and third base, my quivering body willing the ball to come to me, come to me, so I could swoop down and snag a grounder in my glove, rise, throw off my glove which was a righty glove so it was on my left hand which was my throwing hand, wind up my throwing arm, turn and step into the throw and feel the core of my body torque as I let loose a bullet to first base. Out! The shout of the umpire, reverberating inside my drunk-with-pleasure skull.

I'm not sure a ball thrown by a ten year old deserves to be referred to as a bullet, but that's my interpretation of my ten year old self, and I own it.

I felt like such a child-star shortstop that, had I access to the names and addresses of any famous ball players, I would have written a letter and asked them to be my pen pal and swap stories. Fortunately, I lived in the remote B.C. village of Christina Lake, far from big city influences like professional ball teams, or even a minor league, and so the integrity of the bubble of my life affirming self-image was never threatened.

I was one of those lucky kids who could run and throw and hit or kick any kind of ball with ease. The large muscle coordination required to excel in sports was gifted to me by my mother, who also played ball until she, a war time baby, traded her freedom for motherhood. Developing large muscle coordination was easy in the natural playground around the mountain-cradled Christina Lake, especially in the 60's when children were free to roam far and wide without parental supervision. Swimming in the lake, climbing the Monashee Mountains, and chasing and throwing snowballs or rocks at the kid who bullied my brother, these were my training activities.

My success as shortstop on the local girls' softball team induced such a sense of power and possibility that at night in my bed, when my mother was blasting Barbra Streisand's 'I'm Gonna Shine' on the stereo, I would belt it out along with Barbra and feel my heart and dreams soar. I would grow up and play professional softball! When I told my father my plan he said, 'Sorry Mitchell, there's no professional ladies softball teams'. 'Then I'll start my own!' I shouted.

I kept that dream alive until my early teens, at which point life's realities caused its abrupt death. But I have learned that a true dream, one born out of personal belief and joy alone, a dream nurtured without expectations of material gain or peer adulation, a bona fide, genuine dream, never really dies.

As an adult, softball remained my sport of choice. My game. I have played softball and its variant, slo-pitch, all over Canada including on both coasts and in one territory. I have played through the rumble of thunder and the blaze of lightning, under scorching suns, in torrential rain, snow, hail and sleet. On the field I have swatted mosquitoes, flies, wasps, and the giant flesh-ripping beetles of the north. I never missed a game but in order to hold that record, I have shamelessly lied, coerced, begged, and demanded. Intuitively, I understood what had to be done for my team, my game.

But, there was a time, that time when my dream had died, when it took my doctor's orders to get me back in the game.

CHAPTER 1

THE WINTER HAD BEEN LONG AND COLD BUT DRY, WITH AN unrelenting wind that stripped every speck of snow and grain of topsoil from the fields of our southern Alberta acreage, stealing it with the kind of authority thunder steals your nerves. Day after day, I stood at the kitchen window, watching the dirt blast across the fields and our long gravel driveway, yearning and aching for the grey sky to snow or let the sun through. Watching, waiting, I felt that cruel wind ripping and tearing and stealing my soul. I was chronically tired and by 4:00 p.m. each day, wanted to go to bed for the night. At my feet, mega blocks and bubble poppers, toy trucks and trains, and two beautiful blue eyed, darling, sometimes happy sometimes not, little diaper clad boys. Replace the plastic toys with roughhewn wooden blocks and it could have been a scene from Little House on the Prairie. We even had the barn out back. And a root cellar.

I felt I understood something of those poor prairie homesteaders of the Dirty Thirties.

I was having my own Great Depression.

I was 23 years old and working as a full time mother, raising my two sons on a large acreage between Calgary and a small commuter town called Okotoks, in the province of Alberta. Meanwhile, Husband and I were trying to establish a construction company, beginning with one bulldozer that was good for roughing out driveways and digging holes for basements. But it was 1985, Alberta was in a recession and the only holes being dug were in people's dreams of financial security. Therefore, Husband took the time- honoured Canadian path and worked out of town, leaving me and our sons to keep the home fires burning, literally. We sometimes had to resort to a wood stove to stay warm as the 1980's rural power supply wasn't reliable.

I managed all the conventional Mommy duties at a time when women were supposed to be out breaking the glass ceiling. I was a decade behind those 70's ladies who burned their bras and marched on Parliament demanding affirmative action and pay equity. My ten- year- old sensibilities were shocked rather than liberated when, in the early 70's, my grown up cousin, on a family visit from Vancouver to my small BC village, took off her caftan-style top to enjoy the sun on a public beach, bare- breasted. I was still a kid riding my purple banana seat bike hands free on my way to my ball games, feeling as liberated as a freshly hatched butterfly, years away from contemplating the social implications of female public nudity as an expression of liberation.

When that era of mass female resistance began to fade, many of the bra burners became professional working women and mothers, and were discovering the reality of their liberated state — being a Mommy while slugging it out all day on the career ladder is a potent mix, kind of like a Paralyzer without the milk to make it go down smoothly. I, on the other hand, having been a girl and teenager during the frenzy of the women's lib movement of the 70's, did not feel obligated to follow the path of many other mothers of the 80's and instead, identified as a 'Stay At Home Mom', baking oatmeal cookies, hauling diaper pails up and down the stairs, and writing letters to the editor admonishing those women who were scarring their children for life by leaving them in daycares.

At the rural community playgroup where I took my children on Wednesday mornings, mothers argued about their role in the family and in the community. Working mothers were putting their children in daycare to pursue professional careers, but should they be? These same women were still responsible for all the housework, shopping and child care, but should they be? We stay at home moms were footing the tax bill for working mothers, and doing all the community volunteer work, but should we be? While the children threw sand at the sand table, water at the water table, and paint at the paint station, opinions popped, tempers flared.

Invigorating debate, yet the chronic tiredness persisted.

The doctor's order came in April, 1985. I made an appointment to find out if I had a serious illness or just some kind of virus. "I have no energy. I'm tired all the time," I told him. 'I just want to sleep." "I haven't had a fever or anything like that, but it's been going on for months, so I must have some kind of bug."

The doctor was an old hand at his profession. He did the usual thing with those devices doctors use to look in your ears and eyes and listen to your lungs and your heart and then he snapped closed the object hanging around his neck and said. "The only thing wrong with you is you're spending too much time at home taking care of your kids and your husband, and not enough time taking care of yourself. You're depressed. Get out of the house and go do something for yourself."

On the way home from the doctor's office, I realized with brutal, gut twisting clarity that he was right. Even brushing my hair and dressing attractively had become a chore. My outfit of choice was a hideously ugly two piece furry brown number that insulated me from the cold drafts blowing through the cracks of our old house. My furry brown outfit may have been a criminal fashion offense but it was the only outfit that suited my sensibilities at the time. Funny, Husband never said a word about it. But then, in those days Husband didn't say much at all. Never a talker, and perhaps feeling equally shell-shocked with the rapid change from freewheeling adult with money to spend to father of two with a mortgage, a business launched during a recession, and a depressed wife.

Go do something for yourself.

I'd already had the same message in a birthday card from my sister who was at home with a brood of her own. The front of the card had a cartoon drawing of a woman in front of a mirror holding the end of a vacuum nozzle near her neck, upon which a clear mark had been left looking suspiciously like a hickey. Inside, the card read, 'hope you're not suffering from shut- in syndrome'. *Go do something for yourself.*

Within hours, let's say no more than 48, I had made a decision: I dialed the Town of Okotoks office number. The phone rang and rang. Finally, a woman answered:

Woman: Good morning, Town of Okotoks, how can I help you?
Me: Hi, I'm calling to find out if there are any ladies softball teams in Okotoks?
Woman: Yes, there are two ladies leagues in town, slo-pitch and fast pitch.

Fastpitch? Slo-pitch? What was she talking about?

Me: Oh. I only know softball. What exactly is fastpitch and slo-pitch?
Woman: In fastpitch, the ball is pitched fast and straight. In slo-pitch, the ball is pitched kind of high in the air, and slow.

My youngest was crawling around my feet pulling on my pant legs.

Fastpitch sounded like softball, but I had never seen anything like slo-pitch.

Me: So what else is different?
Woman: Well, let's see. The fastball ladies play twice a week. One in- town game and one

> out-of-town game. The slo-pitch gals just play in town once a week. But you should really call the associations to get all the facts. I have the names and numbers of the Presidents of both leagues.

Now we were getting somewhere. With Husband working day and night, one game a week would be enough of a challenge. I put my foot on the keys of the toy piano my second son, Josh, was now banging.

> Me: Can I have the one for the slo-pitch league please?

While I prepared dinner that night, I wondered how I could take time for myself when Husband was working 7 days a week and the budget was skinnier than the yet to come Ralph Klein welfare cheques.

But, through the steam of the boiling potatoes, the doctor's words bubbled up. *You're spending too much time taking care of everyone else and not enough time taking care of yourself. You're depressed. Go do something for yourself.*

Go do something for yourself.

But who'll take care of my kids?

I don't know but if you don't do something, you aren't going to be of any use to your family. A Happy Wife is a Happy Life.

(The Happy Wife line is mine.)

Over dinner that evening, I informed Husband:

> Me: I'm thinking of joining a ball team. The doctor says I need to get out and do something for myself.
>
> Husband: Mmmmm.

Me: What do you think? I arranged to meet up with a team in Okotoks. Tomorrow night. They're called the Rainbows. Funny name, isn't it?

Husband: Silence.
Me: The league in Okotoks just plays once a week. Do you think you could quit work a bit early one night a week?

Husband softly chuckles, takes another bite of ham.

Me: So, I'll take that as agreement, then?

No more fake hickey birthday cards for me.
I joined the Rainbows.

CHAPTER 2

THE RAINBOWS. WHAT KIND OF FEMALE BALL PLAYERS CALL THEMselves the Rainbows? Most ball teams choose names with the intent to intimidate or invoke fear in their opposition. Names like Man Eaters, Dirt Devils, or, with a nod to a popular party drink, the Paralyzers. The Okotoks Ladies Slo-Pitch League was filled with moderately aggressive names such as The Hustlers, The Renegades, the Shooters and the Lariats. There were also the DeWinton Diggers and the DeWinton Dusters, which suggested effort and result. Then there are teams fortunate enough to be sponsored. The Fountain Tire Flyers, the Super Eight Sluggers.

Yet there I was in 1985, joining a ball team called the Rainbows. I would never join a team called, Cleats and Cleavage, or Top Snatch. But Rainbows? The juvenile sort of name a circle of ten-year-old best friends would choose to match their original dance move for their all girl band. Ball players aren't Rainbows. Church ladies who make all the little square and spiral sandwiches for funeral lunches are Rainbows. Ladies who play ball are more like hurricanes, or at least, storms. Why not a name like Summer Storm, or Okotoks Hurricanes, if we had to go with a weather related theme?

When I learned the team's original name was the 'Puckerettes', I realized they had made a drastic improvement with 'The Rainbows'. The 'Puckerettes' was a shot at their hockey puck chasing husbands who took for granted the right to go play hockey and drink beer all winter long, leaving their wives at home, of course, with the kids.

In 1980, the Rainbows decided to launch their own sports odyssey. If their husbands could take off to chase pucks all winter, then they could take off to chase balls all summer. And to make that statement unequivocally clear, they christened themselves the PUCKerettes.

As I said, the name did not generate the kind of respect they were seeking. Thus, as a result of a team dispute about uniform colour, they settled on a multi-coloured shirt and became, The Rainbows.

CHAPTER 3

MY CHILDHOOD SELF-IMAGE OF MY ABILITIES WAS FIRMLY INTACT that spring of 1985, despite my not having played a formal game since 1977, so on tryout day, rather than warming up at home with a round of catch and some hitting practice, I concentrated on my outfit. Instinctually, I felt I needed to identify with the team colours, as if it would increase my chances of being taken into the flock, or tribe, so to speak.

In spite of the dispute over colour in deciding the team name, by 1985, the uniforms were down to two colours - white and kelly green. Unfortunately, the only kelly green in my wardrobe was a pair of socks. Fuzzy knee highs, as hideously ugly as my furry brown number.

Although they were not particularly attractive socks, or even trendy ones with some paisley or striped patterns, they were the right colour. I wore them with a pair of old shorts. If I had worn sweatpants, the green would barely have been noticeable.

Feeling alternating waves of excitement and nervousness, I drove the twenty minutes from my acreage to the designated ball diamond behind the Percy Pegler elementary school in Okotoks. I pulled my 74 Toronado up beside a row of pickup trucks and noticed the group of women on the diamond stop, all heads turned toward the parking lot. After a moment, they went back to throwing balls around the field.

The first thing I noticed was that no one was wearing fuzzy knee high kelly green socks. They were wearing navy blue or grey sweatpants or sweat shorts and white or grey t-shirts, and short white sports socks. Not a single swatch of green. In fact, the only kelly green at the diamond was the grass.

When I was just six feet away from the bench where a few players were gathered, I saw the eyes of a short woman with shoulder length permed blonde hair flash stealthily between my socks and the eyes of the tall woman with dark brown hair who stood next to her.

I pulled up my socks, lifted my chin, took the last step toward them and said:

Me:	Hi, I'm Michele. Is Trudy here?

A woman with short blonde hair nodded.

Trudy:	Michele, glad you made it! I'm Trudy. This is Debbie.
Me:	Thanks for inviting me.
Trudy:	Are you ready to jump in? What position did you say you played?
Me:	Well, I haven't played for a while, but I was always the shortstop.
Trudy:	For now, let's put you somewhere on the infield. What do you think Debbie?
Debbie:	We could do that, but maybe it would be better if you start in the field, since the infield is already set up.

Clearly, this woman was the boss. I looked out to the field. Left and centre were already occupied, and a third player was out there too, behind second.

Me:	– So, I guess I'll go out to right then? (Not RIGHT! Please!)
Debbie:	Sure, you might as well, but do you wanna warm up first? I'll throw with you.

We moved away from the bench and spread apart. Debbie threw me a ball, which I just managed to keep in my glove because the ball was huge. Huge. Before throwing it back, I held it in my hand and looked at it. I had never seen such a big softball. It felt like a watermelon. Not one of those giant watermelons like the ones Saskatchewan Roughriders fans wear on their heads, but more like those new mini ones you get in the stores now. I think they must have been genetically modified for the divorced and single people living alone, who can't get through a regular sized watermelon before it dries out.

> Me: Wow, this is a big ball.
> Debbie: (Laughing) Yeah. Welcome to slo-pitch.

I gripped the melon ball, but my fingers were too short to get all the way around. I threw the ball back to Debbie but it felt unnatural, more like a push than a throw. My wrist didn't snap the way it should. My arm movement felt unwieldy and stiff. What was all this? Throwing a ball had always been so easy. We continued with the big, fat, foreign ball, but my throws felt weak and lame. Catching the ball in my old glove required a twist of my wrist to keep it in the pocket. How would I ever keep this monster from falling out during a fast play? I concentrated on throwing without losing my grip while my stomach lurched around like a toddler just learning to walk.

> Debbie: Are you warm?
> Me: Yeah, thanks. (No, I'm not warm and I don't like this ball!)

On the diamond, the players were in position throwing balls around, waiting for Debbie who seemed to be the captain and coach. When she picked up a bat and rolled a few balls over to home plate, I took my cue and jogged out to *right field*.

Debbie—a good name for the boss of a ball team. All the Debbie's I'd ever known were confident, successful, and…bossy. Okay, Debbie, I thought, as I moved around the field, determining my exact position. *So I'm here, in the back forty of recreational ball. It's gotta be temporary. As soon as you see how I can play, you'll put me where I belong. As for that melon ball, well, clearly it's time Alberta ball players were introduced to the proper ball size. I have one at home. I'll enlighten everyone as soon as possible. Once we're playing with the proper ball, I'll be able to fire the ball like a bullet and then things will get straightened out. Someone like me can't be relegated to right field.*

Any self-respecting shortstop would be offended by a demotion to right field. In recreational ball, right field is the outback. It's the retirement corner for old players who refuse to give up the game. It's the field for players who have never played before. Right fielders are the Mr. Beans of the game. If you are a right fielder reading this, you know what I'm talking about.

Standing out in right field for the first time in my life, I watched Debbie warm up the infield players. The shortstop picked her balls out of the dirt and shot her throws to first with ease. Her bright pink lipstick and blue eyeshadow stood out against the whiteness of the sky. Seriously.

Okay, so I might need to work my way up, prove I'm as good as she is. Second, third, then short.

But the short plump girl at third had lazer vision with her big round eyeglasses, and looked like a pro when she snapped a line drive out of the air and fired it to second.

Trudy was on second. She missed her first grounder but made up for it on the next one with a clean play. When we were discussing where to put me, she had not suggested I go to *her* position.

Debbie started hitting to the outfield. She sent a deep fly to left. The left fielder jogged casually sideways, catching the ball with the style of a veteran from the American Baseball League; when they trot lazily toward the ball, that demeanor that calls out, *There aint no way this ball is going anywhere but into my glove,* guaranteed, so batter, you might as well park your sorry ass back down on the bench right now. By the time my turn came I was sucking the last of my ego's oxygen in order to concentrate on a clean catch. The relief I felt when I caught my one practice fly, and followed it up with an acceptable throw to first, was so great that had I suffered from incontinence, I would have needed a fresh Depends.

Fortunately, I did not have to repeat the performance. I was called in for some batting practice.

I selected a bat while the pitcher warmed up, felt a surge of power course through me, that familiar shot of adrenalin I had always felt with the bat in my hands. I loved hitting and was good at it; line drives were my specialty and I usually made it to second on my hits, and had plenty of triples and home runs on my record. In regular softball the pitch comes straight and fast, so, as I watched the pitcher toss the peculiar lobs of slo-pitch, I thought, *if I can't be the shortstop right away, at least I'll be a star hitter. Batting in this game will be child's play. I'll be making home runs every time I'm up to bat.*

I chose a 28 ouncer with a medium grip and began swinging it gently back and forth, the traditional warm up, an opportunity to show the opposition how cool you feel, how in control you'll be in the batter's box. As I took my practice swings and watched the pitcher, I felt my confidence build. I felt my arms and legs and feet tingle. I felt strong, fast, invincible.

I stepped up to the plate, placed just one foot in the batter's box, the way serious players do, players with intent, players with a strategy. Slowly, deliberately, I scanned the field, to convey the message that, since I could hit it wherever I wanted, I was selecting the precise piece of grass upon which the ball would land.

The pitcher lobbed in the first ball, which arced high into the air before beginning its descent toward me. My body quivered, my toes danced inside my Reeboks, my hands squeezed the bat and I chose the exact moment to stretch my lead leg forward and wind up for the swing and hit that ball out of the park.

And then I missed. How could I have missed? The pitch was slow and fat as a melon. I looked around but no one else was laughing and the pitcher was waiting for me to get back in the box.

I stepped up to the plate again. Watched the pitcher set up her next pitch, kept my eye on the ball as it rose into the air, watched it gracefully arc over and across the shale between the pitcher's mound and home plate, watched it slowly dropping down toward me, watched it neatly begin its entry into my strike zone, felt my clean swing and heard the thud. Of the ball hitting the ground.

Debbie:	Move up in the batter's box. You're standing too far back.
First Base:	You're crowding the plate too. Give yourself more room.

What plate? It was a ridiculous piece of carpet big enough for a downward dog. Not that anyone had heard of a downward dog in 1985.

I stepped back up to the giant mat for one more try. As the ball approached I shimmied around the mat, lining up for a hit, not caring if the pitch was worth swinging at, only concerned with regaining my dignity.

Ah, the sound of bat meeting ball. Finally! I dropped my bat and ran like my life depended on it, racing the ball which was piddling along next to the first base line, slow as a snowball going uphill.

Inexplicably, at the end of the practice, they invited me to join the team.

That night, in the dark quiet of my bedroom, I wondered who was sleeping in my bed. Who was this person who couldn't hit a pitch lobbed the way parents lob pitches to their five-year-olds? Where did the other person go, the one who could hit the fastest pitch out of the park time after time?

The evening was warm, through my open window came the sound of thousands of frogs singing in a nearby slough. Moonlight and new leaves on the poplars whispered in the breeze.

And it struck me. My glory days of ball were a long time ago. Ten years, to be exact. I had last played in a softball league in Watson Lake, Yukon, when I was thirteen years old. I was a kid. I was the shortstop for the ladies team. There wasn't a girls' team in town at the time.

Outside an owl hooted. Had I really been the player I believed myself to be? Did I really fire off bullets, or were they more like darts, or worse, balloons flying erratically as they deflated? How sure was I about my batting record? How many home runs did I actually get? Doubt wove its way through the moonlight, silenced the frog chorus, and snuck into the shrinking bubble of my self-image. I fell asleep wondering if I should take up something easier, like lawn bowling.

But the next morning, my little sons re-ignited my optimism. And reminded me of my doctor's orders.

I decided I would go back and try again.

CHAPTER 4

When you meet a woman who seems to have her life moving in exactly the direction she wants, you may wonder how to relate to her. Do you look up to her as a mentor and hope some of her self-assurance will rub off on you? Do you reveal your soft uncertain underbelly and hope she will offer protection and guidance? Or do you pull up your shaky socks, look her square in the eye, and try to look like a woman equally advanced along the road to self-actualization?

PLAYER PROFILE
DEBBIE
5'7", 140 lbs.
Junior High French Teacher

Position on the field:
Centre/Right Field, Catcher
Position off field:
Team Captain and Whip
Favourite Phrase:
"Jesus Christ, what now?'
What Debbie wanted:
For the Rainbows to shine forever.

Debbie was almost a decade older than me, and a resolute example of the liberated women of the 70's. She knew exactly what she wanted and had the confidence to go ahead and get it. She was far ahead of many of her peers because she suffered no illusions about who she was and what made her happy. She was married to a successful farmer and rancher and had two children. She was a natural community leader and a respected (some might say feared) teacher of French to the toughest level of education – junior high students, many generations of whom she led on trips to France, a miraculous feat. She was the undisputed Yoda of the Okotoks Ladies Slo-Pitch Association, the Okotoks Ladies Curling Association, the Hockey Parents Association, the How to Organize Anything Association. She drank white wine with ice and did not apologize for it.

So how did I approach this hero, this queen, this chief player and doer? As a woman of wisdom and vision, naturally. Early and often while enjoying post game refreshments I expounded on threats and issues, such as irradiated food, or nuisance by-laws. This tactic, I felt, would put me on an equal footing with this woman who, I learned later, had long figured out the futility of worrying about things over which she had no control. Despite this, she tolerated my ramblings with a respectful mix of silence and 'yeahs' and allowed me the illusion that I knew what I was talking about.

Important note: Debbie did not always give this gift of patience to other Rainbows, most of whom were her chronological peers. For them, a more typical response to a rant on social issues was, "Oh for chrissakes, shutup and have another drink'.

Debbie was the 'founding mother' of the Rainbows. And like any good mother, she set a high standard for herself and everyone else. Because she herself would not be late or miss a game for anything less pressing than a death in the family, this expectation was a hard one to meet. Debbie arranged her calendar from May through September to accommodate the ball season.

Family reunions, weddings, and if possible funerals, could not be scheduled without first consulting with Debbie's game and tournament schedule. Vacations were taken in winter. Husbands were irrelevant. Their job was to take care of the kids when we played ball. Heaven help one of them if they caused a Rainbow grief, for Debbie's wrath would descend upon them without mercy. It was like Tom Clancy's, The Firm. Tom Cruise would have understood.

TRUDY WAS ANOTHER FOUNDING MEMBER OF THE RAINBOWS WHO came with the added bonus of a coach – her husband. Significantly, this relationship did not bestow on her any advantages; not once did I see her receive special treatment. At games, anyway. In fact, Trudy and her husband maintained a professional distance

PLAYER PROFILE
TRUDY
5'3", 130 lbs.
Banker

Position on the field:
Second Base
Position off field:
Team Treasurer
Favourite Phrase:
"Man, do I ever need a coffee'
What Trudy wanted:
A tax deduction for coffee.

from each other during games, which I completely credited to their desire to appear fair, until they split up. Theirs' was the first divorce I had 'seen' in my life at that point, and I was impressed with their civility toward each other and their consideration for all those people around them. They were a model divorced couple and Trudy was a model second basewoman. Unless she had started her day without a cup of coffee.

Trudy held the position of second base until she left the Rainbows in the mid 90's. Her departure was a surprise and somewhat of a blow to Debbie, who believed that as one of the founding members, Trudy was equally committed to guiding the team to athletic glory, in so far as amateur athletes can achieve the glory that becomes a legacy of stories for great great grandchildren and, perhaps, the entire world. Despite this expectation, after her divorce, Trudy did leave the Rainbows. For a man. Which, from the view of this collection of liberated 70's ladies, was incomprehensible. However, Trudy's decision was respected, and she continued to attend the Rainbow's Annual Windup Banquets/Roasts as a guest, bringing along her new man.

In losing Trudy, Debbie lost her right hand, since Trudy was also a natural organizer and administrator and alternated with Debbie as team rep on the local Ladies Slo-Pitch Association executive. When Trudy wasn't working with Debbie to organize the annual Okotoks Ladies Slo-pitch Association Invitational Tournament, she was tracking down prices on new bats and balls, or handling the team's funds, or collecting deposits from players for one of our national tours. (I like to call our trips to national slo-pitch competitions our 'national tours'. Doesn't it sound good?) Through all these activities, Trudy had her go-cup of coffee at hand. She could have been a poster girl for the trend—a true, dedicated, go-cupper.

IN MY VIEW, A TEAM OF COMICS WEIGHTED HEAVILY WITH CYNICS and smartasses is not complete without one comic dedicated to slapstick. The Rainbows complement of comics was gifted with one and her name was Darlene. Only Darlene would actually hang from her ears and neck a dyed green tampon jewelry set. Only Darlene would proudly display on her ample bosom the sunflower seed shells that didn't make it past that barrier when she spit them out. Only Darlene would stand before hundreds of National Championship fans and demonstrate a camp song that requires one to arrange one's arms and arse in awkward and embarrassing poses.

Darlene was our team clown, a great pitcher, and a good friend. When we weren't playing ball together we often gathered our kids up, a total of six between the two of us, and took them on field trips to see 15 foot long pythons, 30 foot high dinosaur skeletons, or buffalo jumps. During these outings Darlene rarely adopted

PLAYER PROFILE
DARLENE
5'6", 140 lbs.
Mother of 3 boys, Entrepreneur

Position on the field:
Pitcher
Position off field:
  Dedicated wife and mother
Favourite Phrase:
"Will"
What Darlene wanted:
Will Will Will Will Will.

her clown persona because we were busy educating our children. She saved her performances for campfires and adult only events.

There is only one other thing to be said about Darlene.
Will Will Will Will Will.
Will is Darlene's husband.
Once more for old time's sake:
Will Will Will Will Will.

CHAPTER 5

THE NEW WOMAN ON THE TEAM OFTEN SITS OUT MOST OF EACH game on the bench for weeks before finally getting to play more than the last inning when there is little risk of messing up a victory plainly in sight.

I played my first game with the Rainbows in early May, 1985. I spent the entire game on the bench with a pulled and throbbing vastus intermedius, a vast but as opposed to intermediate, advanced injury I sustained at the tryout the week before.

If you really want to know where the vastus intermedius is located, you can look it up.

CHAPTER 6

STARTING MY SLO-PITCH CAREER WITH A PULLED VASTUS INTERmedius was portentous, but I didn't know it at the time. In fact, I didn't really see it in that light for at least ten years. I was only shocked that muscles I had taken for granted were capable of such treachery. I'm still surprised and disappointed when my body refuses to do what I ask it to do, but in these intervening years, other muscles and parts of my skeletal system have betrayed me far worse than did my vastus intermedius, so I have had to learn, like so many other unexpected twists and turns in life, to let it go.

My vastus intermedius did heal and I did start learning how to properly hit a slo-pitch pitch. Throwing the melon ball, however, was a constant challenge. And so was child care.

Despite the liberating 70's, in the 1980's, most married women with or without children, were still taking care of most, if not all, of the housework and childcare, even if they were working an additional job outside the home. This was the era of the 'Superwoman', or 'Supermom', when women were frantically pursuing careers or post-secondary education while still accepting responsibility for all domestic related work.

I confess. I was a Supermom.

With fierce pride I read to, played with, fed and washed my sons, cleaned, scrubbed, and scraped all unwanted waste, bacteria and soil from home and garden, washed and hung out to dry in the fresh country air every sock, sheet, and reusable plastic bag, shopped weekly for food items needed for three well balanced meals and two snacks per day, and managed the household budget.

I also grew, harvested, blanched, froze, and canned pure, nutritious, pesticide and herbicide free, organic food that did not have to be transported to our kitchen table in a carbon producing vehicle. (carbon counting and the 100 mile diet had not yet been invented so I guess I was ahead of that curve). At night, I began studying and writing essays for an ever elusive university degree. Meanwhile, Husband worked most days' dawn to dusk, digging holes and hauling dirt with our first bulldozer and dump truck. Child care was not a day to day matter as I was the prime caregiver and damn proud of it.

But on ball nights, since Husband was rarely home early enough to take care of the children, I needed a sitter. I made arrangements with a neighbor and friend from our (day time only) babysitting co-op. Terrill had two babysitting- aged sons whose only shortcomings were their lack of driver's licenses. Since they were ages 12 and 13, there was nothing that could legally be done about that. However, in the country, a neighbour was anyone who lived within twenty miles of our acreage, and, since these neighbours lived only a mile away, I was grateful for them. I might have suggested they walk over if not for the high speed transportation corridor that had to be crossed, and the quarter mile long stretch of dirt road that was guarded by an ornery Texas longhorn bull. Due to these challenges, it was expected that I would drive over and pick up the boys. So, on game nights, arranging childcare went something like this:

In the morning, call neighbour:

Me:	Hi Terrill, I've got a game tonight, I'll need to be in Okotoks by 6. Can one of the boys babysit if Husband doesn't make it home in time?
Terrill:	I think so, what time will you be here?
Me:	5:10, but I will call first to confirm.

4:45 p.m. Dial Terrill's number:

Me: Hi. I haven't seen Husband all day so can you get one of the boys ready?

4:55 p.m. Now in my uniform, I throw my ball bag into the back of my 1974 teal blue Toronado, give my boys each a homemade peanut butter oatmeal (but not sugar free), cookie, strap them into their car seats and get the car in the go position.
5:00: p.m. Call Terrill:

Me: I'm leaving now, be there in 7 minutes!
Terrill: Do you want me to send Stephen down to the gate?
Me: That would be great, thanks!

If the ornery Texas longhorn bull was standing in the middle of the driveway, had Google been photographing southern Alberta from space in 1985, it would have captured the image of a teal blue '74 Toronado going nose to nose with a bull sporting a 15 foot long set of horns, and a thick as pumpernickel bread kelly green pants clad woman standing next to the teal blue 74 Toronado waving a Louisville Slugger baseball bat at the beast. Sometimes, on my way to pick up the babysitter, Husband, driving the dump truck and hauling the bulldozer, would miraculously appear on the horizon. Quickly, I would make a calculation: the drive directly from my acreage to the ball diamond was 17 minutes provided I wasn't stopped for speeding. The time to turn my '74 Toronado around and return to the acreage was variable. Once back on home territory, I needed at least 8 minutes to find Husband amongst the old broken cars, buses and snowmobiles, farm machinery and piles of scrap steel, get his attention, release the boys into his care, and inform him he was from that moment solely responsible for their safety and well-being. And of course, supper was in the fridge. In addition, since this is pre-cell phone era, I had to go into the house and contact my neighbour to call the babysitting off. If Terrill had already sent babysitter to gate and then gone out to her garden to harvest her tender baby zucchinis, the phone call would go unanswered and I would be facing a moral dilemma. Do I leave babysitter stranded at the gate in order to make the game on time, or do I arrive late at the game and save babysitter and Terrill the trouble of launching a rescue mission in case I had been impaled on a Texas longhorn?

Depending on my decision, I would either arrive on time and take up my position in right field, or I would arrive late and suffer Debbie's reprimand. "Jesus Christ, wouldn't it be easier to just bring them with you?"

Bringing my sons to my games was always an option, but, being a forerunner to the helicopter parent era, I was not prepared to have my two preschoolers off playing in a playground an entire field away from adult supervision. Our team rover, Kerry, was often without a babysitter and I felt her anxiety as she watched for balls coming at her while keeping an eye on her boys on the next field over. I did not have that kind of fortitude. I would be knocked unconscious by the one ball that might come out to right field. I would wake up and find my boys abducted. And worse, I would miss out on the post-game beers.

Post-game beers, after all, were an essential part of my doctor's orders. And the Rainbows had a well-established tradition, along with all the other ball teams in town, of taking a post-game beer at the Lazy L.

The Lazy L was a first generation sports bar, and, although the sport it venerated most was rodeo, all the local ball players patronized it because it was the only sports style pub in town. For the first decade or so of Rainbows history, our post game socializing happened at the Lazy L.

The name Lazy L may have referred to a cattle brand, or it may have referred to the name of the pub owner, which was

Lester. Unlike bars in other southern Alberta towns like, Picture Butte, or Whiskey Gap, Lester's dark and highly polished wooden bar did not sport any tobacco chewing dudes hiking up their rope totin' Wranglers. By the 1980's, most of the farmer types bellying up to Lester's bar just chewed on steaks and the "god damn Crow Rate." But the bar did sport plenty of other western style artifacts, such as coin operated pool tables surrounded by walls filled with frame after frame of autographed photos of local rodeo heroes captured in life- threatening dramas: a bull rider being tossed in the air, or a rodeo clown hiding behind a plastic barrel while a raging bull paws at the ground and snorts. The picture didn't come with video so you couldn't actually hear the bull snorting, but you could imagine it. When you live in rural southern Alberta, it's easy to imagine the sound of bulls snorting because you can go to a rodeo in almost any town and hear one, up close and personal, if you like that kind of thing.

During a typical post game visit to Lester's, my team would settle around a group of high top tables, hooking our cleats on the stool rail while the server delivered the standard complimentary pitchers of draft beer. Sherry and Kathy filled the glasses while others ordered chicken wings or steak sandwiches. Debbie might have been having a tizzy about not enough players joining in on the post-game socializing. Meanwhile, I was digging around in my wallet for a coin for the pay phone. If I took one sip of beer before calling home to check on my children, the beer would get stuck in my throat. This is one of the many, many, many, ways in which motherly guilt is manifested.

In those pre-cell phone days, mothers did not have the option of calling home or texting in ten minute increments to assuage their conscience. Instead, we had to use the pay phone. The delineation line between mothers who had freed themselves of, or had never suffered under, the yoke of guilt, was drawn by a line of lady ball players, yoked mothers like myself, who were all standing dutifully, one behind the other, waiting to make the call that would either result in one last hour of respite, or a premature conclusion of our time out. While waiting my turn, I gaped in envious wonder at the Rainbows mothers like Sherry and Debbie, who allowed themselves the full pleasure of every second of their recreational time. Maya Angelou would have admired them. As Maya said, "….I've been female for a long time now. I'd be stupid not to be on my own side."

A call home would sound something like this:

Me:	Hi, are the kids in bed?
Husband:	Yep.
Me:	Great, I'll see you in an hour or two then.

Or…

Husband:	Nope.
Me:	Where are they?
Husband:	I'm not sure, actually.
Me:	What!!?? How can you not know where they are?
Husband:	Well, they're in the house here somewhere, I'm trying to round them up.
Me:	Have they had their bath yet?

If the answer to this crucial question was no, my post-game beer would be off. If the answer was yes, there was hope.

Secrets from Lester's Lazy L:

IF WALLS COULD SPEAK, THOSE AT LESTER'S LAZY L WOULD HAVE A lot of stories to tell. Recorded in their layers of paint and drywall were some of the Rainbows most historic off the field moments, such as when Debbie allowed herself to get carried away on her birthday and over imbibed in a popular drink at that time – the paralyzer. On one of only two occasions when I saw Debbie succumb to temptation, on this evening, she felt compelled to rest for a moment on the pool table. Her husband thought she would be more comfortable at home and so, he leaned over his stricken wife and said, "I think I should take you home now Debra". To which Debbie replied, "I always go home with whoever I came with and I came with Kerry."

Later, reflecting on that conspicuous night, Karen remarked: "Jesus Christ, we drank so many paralyzers we stamped out osteoporosis in one night!"

CHAPTER 7

KAREN SHOULD HAVE BEEN A RADIO HOST. HER DISTINCT VOICE sounded like a French horn with fine sand in the works. When Karen was pleased, her voice would rise with her exclamatory 'No Shit!' – for example, when she was told that someone had just treated her to a vodka and seven. When we were losing to a team like the Man Eaters and I said to her, 'we need to get on our bats'. Karen turned her huge brown eyes to me and with a plummet of several octaves delivered her 'No shit', so dark and

PLAYER PROFILE
KAREN
5'6", 130 lbs.
Business Owner and Accountant

Position on the field:
Third Base
Position off field:
Team Comic and Pharmacist
Favourite Phrase:
'No Shit'
What Karen wanted:
A live-in babysitter.

flat it froze the air between us, and my heart. Karen had that kind of effect on people.

To keep up with a woman like Karen, one required a sharp eye for the humour and irony of life. Unfortunately, as a young Rainbow my eye was still trained more on social injustice than social comedy, and therefore I frequently missed her outbursts of humour, most of which came as a reaction to life's continual stream of uncontrolled variables that caused her to arrive at games in a rush, or miss games or tournaments altogether. Uncontrolled variables in Karen's life: her husband showing up when she didn't need him or not showing up when she did, customers either showing up or not showing up when they were not supposed to or supposed to, the family dog disappearing, one of the kids disappearing, or getting pregnant.

Karen's response to any of these circumstances would be to arrive at the diamond, sit down on the bench and smoke a cigarette. On some days she smoked the cigarette in a folded position – bent over, arms resting on knees, head down. Just her and the smoke. Occasionally she would look up and around and say "Well just look at you, all bouncy bouncy. Christ." Eventually, she would straighten up and if Debbie was within earshot, plead, 'How about I stick to the bench tonight Deb?'

On better days she would arrive at the game, take the bench, light a cigarette, pull one leg up across the other and to the first Rainbow available and the conversation would go something like this:

Karen:	So how the hell are ya?
Me:	Fine, how about you?
Karen:	Oh, I'm pretty good, pretty good…(then a slight pause)
	Got a sore foot though. Tripped over the god damn vacuum cleaner this morning when I got up. Christ, that was some

surprise. Thought I had left the thing leaning against the wall by the window last night.

I waited, sure there was more, some kind of a punchline.

Karen: Do you believe in ghosts Michele?

I laughed, and Karen laughed too, but only for half a beat.

Karen: No really, I'm not kidding. There's a god damn ghost living in my house. I'm sure of it.
Me: Maybe Barry used the vacuum and left it there.
Karen: Ha! Barry? Vacuum? I'll put my money on my ghost.

On the diamond Karen played third base until her knees gave out. Her knees were ruined from too many years of basketball. She gave up basketball for slo-pitch, and eventually gave up slo-pitch for golf. In the 80's when your knees gave out you didn't get a new set, you got a new sport. When her first two children were both teenagers and her third was starting elementary school, Karen got pregnant, the biggest surprise of all. She left the Rainbows soon after, to enjoy her beautiful new daughter and salvage what she could of her knees.

She continued to show up at games periodically and always attended our annual windup. Her storytelling is legendary. She is the kind of person everyone wants at a party. When I sat down to visit with Karen last, she opened up with a fairly serious topic.

Karen: Hey Michele, long time no see. How ya' been?
Me: Good Karen, how about you?

Karen:	Oh, you know, same shit, different day. So what are you doing these days? You working? Had any more kids? We laughed together. We had our last within a year of each other, long, long, after the rest of the team had finished with babies.
Me:	You know, just taking care of the WIRE office and still on the MD Council.

By this time, I had become an elected official in the rural municipality in which we lived.

Karen:	So what's that like? I've always wondered how you manage with all those old farts. Christ, some of them should have died by now, don'tcha think?

I was the only woman on the Council, and the only member not in the category of senior citizen.

Me:	Yeah, they're definitely on the senior side of things. But most of them are pretty sharp.
Karen:	Christ, Barry and I were in there for a hearing once, this was before your time, and we swore one of them had up and died in his chair. We were there for an hour and he didn't move once. I wanted to poke him but Barry wouldn't let me. Turns out he was just sleeping. Made me mad, but then I realized as long as he's sleeping he can't do any damage.'

ON THE FIELD, KERRY HAD A CALM AND RESULTS DRIVEN APPROACH to the game that I envied. She also possessed an astounding array of practical skills, some of which I was trying my best to acquire. Such as cooking huge quantities of delicious home baked beans, pies, and other classic prairie farm specialties. And managing her two children effectively but without a lot of fuss. She could do a lot of other things extremely well, including saddling up and riding a horse and delivering cows, but I wasn't aiming that high.

When Kerry wasn't pulling wet and bloody calves from the birth canals of bawling cows, or fixing fences knocked down by horny bulls, or galloping across the field on her horse to rope an errant steer, or shoveling shit from the horse corral into her garden patch, or corralling her two boys into the bathtub, or doing the books for the family farm—she was playing ball. Seriously. Kerry did all that and more. Much more, since she was also the Rainbows designated driver.

PLAYER PROFILE
KERRY
5'4", 120 lbs.
Farmer, mother of 2

Position on the field:
Rover
Position off field:
DD
Favourite Phrase:
"I don't know"
What Kerry wanted:
I don't know.

Kerry was a low maintenance player. She was always on time and ran the bases well. She never bothered with hats, or sunglasses, or batting gloves and although she had a favourite bat, if for some reason it was unavailable she managed just as well with another one. She never needed a Tylenol and was usually in a good mood. When she arrived at our weekly games and I asked her how she was her stock answer was 'Good!' When I asked her how the crops were doing, I got, "Good, I think, but you'd have to ask Jack". If I asked her if she would make the next out- of- town tournament, she would answer, 'I hope so, but I don't know, we're pretty busy right now'. Her non-committal approach was not a sign of indecision or lack of interest, but rather a keen appreciation of the curve balls life can throw. Would a horse get ripped up in barbed wire and need to go to the vet? Would her babysitter come through? Would she get all the garden beans and peas harvested in time? Would the branding be wrapped up? Would the contractor show up as planned to fix the leaky roof? Would there be a crop failure? A husband failure? A child emergency?

These uncontrolled variables in her life kept her ready and alert and sober. Rarely did Kerry imbibe in alcohol. Her drink of choice was plain soda, and so she was a reliable DD and often the personal driver of our team captain, Debbie, whose home was on her route to and from town.

Cows, horses, children, husband, ball games, all were treated with her steady competent hand, her quiet confidence, her determination to do things well and make progress on each and every day.

The only exception to her otherwise composed approach to life was when she was trying for the first time to make pie crust. Her high standards required her to make excellent pie crust. Better than Tender Flake's, better than Simple Simon's, better than a Parisian patisserie. Although by the 80's a female farmer was technically exempt from having to produce award winning pies, there were undoubtedly still many women on farms who suffered from a lingering sense of wifely or domestic obligation to be able to produce pies that would win a ribbon at an agricultural fair. Fortunately, this was not the case with Kerry. She wanted only to satisfy herself. If she could not find the 25th hour in the day to make a homemade pie, she would do the practical thing and go to Costco. In fact, the gravel roads of the agricultural region south of Calgary regularly suffered the weight and ripping up of hundreds of half ton pickup trucks returning from 'the city', loaded with $1000.00 worth of Costco pies, buns, sandwich meat, steaks and potatoes, cheese and sausage. And the women driving those trucks were always, always, speeding because they always, always, had to be somewhere. In Kerry's case, often a ball game.

But back to the pie crust.

Kerry had set aside a few hours one summer evening to make her first scratch crust. She had the recipe, the lard, the flour and the confidence needed to attempt homemade pastry. She combined the ingredients and began to pat out a mound of dough on the flour dusted counter. But the mound of dough was as hard as a softball and wouldn't flatten out despite a good pounding, so she dropped it in the garbage. To improve her next batch she added additional water, but the result was a ball of slime. Into the garbage.

Hours passed, the robins outside the window began their late evening serenade, the scent of ripening hay wafted, and the garbage can filled with wads of rejected pastry. A thunderstorm chased her boys in and across the kitchen floor in muddy shoes. Kerry didn't notice. She was deep into battle with pastry.

At midnight, she snapped. Instead of doing a drop shot into the garbage, she fired the pastry ball at the furthest wall. The next failed batch hit the same spot. Kerry had a mean shot.

Around 2:00 AM, Jack, got in from the fields, or the pub, I'm not sure on that point. As he took in the scene, he sniffed the kitchen air. "Something smells really good."

'It better smell good". Sit down and eat". Jack didn't dare argue. He sat down at the kitchen table and ate the best pie with the most superb crust that he had ever tasted. And Jack had eaten a lot of pie.

Jack could have gained a lot of brownie points that night had he offered to clean up the kitchen, but there was Kerry when the robins began their morning wakeup call, scraping her temper tantrum off the wall. Alone, but immensely satisfied with her results.

As a ball player, Kerry applied the same standard to her game. She was our Rover, a position that allowed her to move anywhere in the outfield. Her favourite spot was behind second base where she could nab line drives or grounders coming up the middle and fire off the ball to whichever base called for the play. However, if a heavy hitter was up to bat and Debbie felt Kerry wasn't showing enough respect for the potential for a deep fly, she had to shout, "BACK UP!" Kerry would pretend not to hear. But Debbie, not to be defied, would shout louder and reluctantly, Kerry would step backwards again, until Debbie stopped shouting. We no longer had a rover, but instead four fielders. From right field I could see Kerry's lips tighten and her nostrils flare. I could see her bare left hand feeling the pocket of her glove, and I imagined her shaping it, getting it ready to receive a ball. Her stance, straight, feet side by side, bare hand inside the pocket of her glove, her eyes trained like lazers on the batter at home plate. When the ball came her way she was on the move and with Debbie yelling, "BACK BACK BACK" I knew Kerry was whispering, "oh shit" as she turned and ran for the ball.

CHAPTER 8

Me:	There's a tournament in Claresholm next month.
Husband:	Oh yeah.
Me:	The team's going down Friday since our first game is early Saturday morning. The final is Sunday.
Husband:	Mmmm.
Me:	The team needs to know if I'm coming.
Husband:	Oh yeah.
Me:	I'd like to go. If we make the final, we probably won't be back until dinner time Sunday.
Husband:	Oh yeah.
Me:	So you can stay home with the boys for the weekend? Or should I ask my parents to take them?

I chose to interpret Husband's faint, mysterious laughter as acquiescence and to his complete surprise departed on Friday night after giving him written instructions regarding mealtimes, bedtimes, naptimes, bathtimes, and storytimes. Soon after closing the door and settling into the backseat of Debbie's suburban, I discovered a stowaway in my overnight bag and her name was Guilt.

Guilt was an overbearing and intrusive companion that appeared soon after I started to enjoy myself with the Rainbows. Guilt nagged inside my head; *what makes you think you should be having fun, hiring babysitters, shirking your responsibilities, spending money on yourself.* I would throw the Doctor's Orders back at her; *go do something for yourself, go do something for yourself!* GO DO SOMETHING FOR YOURSELF!

Guilt rode with me when I drove to regular games. I ripped up the gravel road to Highway 552, my Michael Jackson eight track blaring. But my stereo didn't have the capacity to drown out Guilt's constant refrain. *You shouldn't be going to the game. You shouldn't be taking a night off. You shouldn't be asking Husband and neighbours and Texas Longhorns to accommodate you. You shouldn't. You shouldn't. You shouldn't.*

To ease Guilt's damage to my conscience, I avoided all other forms of girl fun, like shopping, manicures, and the pursuit of a professional career. Instead, I unleashed a full on assault on Guilt. Guilt could only shrink in awe as I stocked my two gigantic deep freezers with the bounty from my Hutterite- sized garden, and mowed and whipper- snipped grass and thistles off five acres of yard, and chopped dandelions down to the root with my garden spade so the American Goldfinches that fed on them would not be poisoned by the Roundup that would have made the job so much easier. I dared Guilt to look through the windows I cleaned inside and out every month to rid them of bug poop and dust. I dared her to dispute the authenticity of my commitment to the betterment of my community, volunteering for anything anyone suggested. I was, as I've mentioned, a Supermom.

Yet, despite all my efforts and the extra large pot of nutrient dense homemade soup prepared for the weekend, there in my lap during the entire 58 minute drive from Okotoks to Claresholm, was Guilt. She was relentless. She came up again and again, like rhubarb. In Claresholm, she squeezed beside me in my lawn chair at the bbq on Friday night, and later, snuggled up beside me in bed.

In the morning she hung around the room like a strumpet after a long and satisfying night. But I refused to let her follow me out the door. There was a barrier around the diamond, and it was redemptive. Every time I stepped onto the shale and grass of a ball diamond I felt as though I had entered a field of grace, a sense of being in exactly the place I was meant to be. Since a ball diamond is not set up for permanent residence, I had to run the gauntlet every time I left my home and children to get to a game.

Warming up that Saturday morning, the Big Sky country around Claresholm brought me relief. Claresholm is in the middle of farm country in Southern Alberta. Beyond the ball diamond and recreational park were crops readying for harvest, and endless miles of grass upon which beef cattle grazed, fattening themselves in ignorant bliss. Under that big blue sky I breathed in that pure uncomplicated air that affirmed my place and fed my soul.

But that was only during the warmup. I started out the game on the bench where I sat with our scorekeeper, Ruth. Ruth impressed me. She seemed a woman who really had control over her own mind and emotions, a woman who had easily reconciled the challenges of her personal obligations to her family with her right to her own recreation time, much of which she spent with the Rainbows. She had already raised her own daughters so she didn't need to mother any of us, which suited everyone just fine. But, if I felt disappointed, or frustrated, or nervous, she always had a few words to let me know she understood.

Unlike paid professional scorekeepers who sit under sun shelters in padded chairs with backs and have cool drinks delivered to them and track scores with electronic computerized devices, Ruth sat on hard benches with no back support in sweltering sun or hail, sleet, or rain, keeping score in a paper scorebook with a pen. And despite never receiving a pay cheque for this service, Ruth never missed a game. This was commitment.

Ruth also could be relied on to deliver a running commentary on the lives of her girls and her grandchildren while keeping an indisputably exact score of the game. If anyone challenged Ruth's record of the score she defended it....well, ruthlessly. So certain was she of the accuracy of her records she would, if necessary, delay games in order to compare notes with the opposition's scorekeeper and, if necessary, call upon the tournament organizers to argue her points. I guess when you're a senior citizen you can adopt such tactics without fear of a backlash. Who would dare to argue with a slight but ram rod straight backed grey- haired lady with pink lipstick and a touch of blush, dressed in neatly pressed pants, a sparkling sweatshirt, and a matching set of earrings and necklace?

For twenty years Ruth was a passionate supporter of the Rainbows. Willing to suffer cranky husbands, argumentative umpires and other scorekeepers, rotten weather, and the occasional whining Rainbow, she never, ever, let us down. All Ruth asked in return was that we listen to her chatter and express her pride in the other girls in her life, the ones to whom she'd given birth and the girls they gave birth to. They were Ruth's joyful world when she wasn't keeping score for the Rainbows.

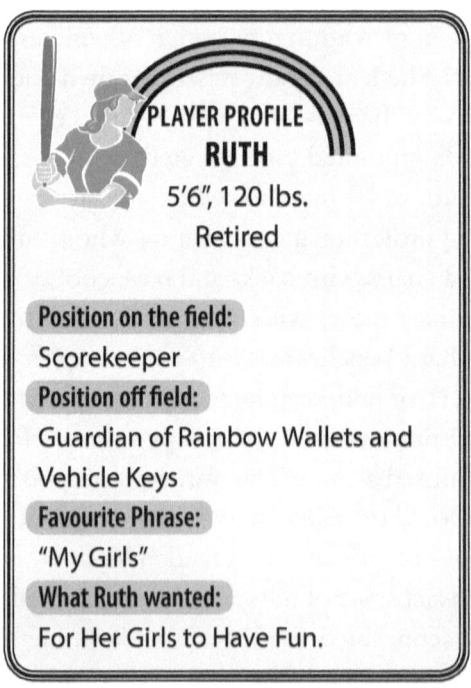

PLAYER PROFILE
RUTH
5'6", 120 lbs.
Retired

Position on the field:
Scorekeeper

Position off field:
Guardian of Rainbow Wallets and Vehicle Keys

Favourite Phrase:
"My Girls"

What Ruth wanted:
For Her Girls to Have Fun.

Ruth passed away in 2016. At her memorial service the Rainbows caught up on the lives of her daughters and granddaughters. I noticed all her offspring had, like their mother and grandmother, developed their own distinct sense of style, and, like Ruth, had grabbed whatever life offered them and made the most of it. Ruth and her legacy have stayed with me, and I am a better person for it

BACK IN CLARESHOLM, CONDITIONS WERE PERFECT FOR A BALL game. Cool calm air, clear morning light. The team looked sharp. Darlene's sky high lobs were sinking the opponent's efforts to score deep hard hits, and when a batter did connect, the ball sailed high in the sky over left field, where Sonny roamed. She would saunter under those flies and wait for them to drop into her glove.

On the bench I slid my hand into my glove for the tenth time. Sensing my frustration, Ruth reassured me. "Slo-pitch is a different game from fast pitch, and these girls have been together for a few years now. Your turn will come. It's good to just be here. I don't get away from home much. Gord doesn't think he can manage without me, but my daughters always help me out when I need a break. Sometimes Gord complains about all the time I spend with the Rainbows but that's too bad for him, I won't let down my girls…"

I hoped Ruth was right. Although I had adjusted my batting technique to the slow pitch and, with some nice solid line drives, recovered my dignity as a batter, there was still the matter of the size of the ball. My throws were okay, but far from what they needed to be to make it to shortstop. My hand wasn't going to get any bigger, and apparently, the ball wasn't going to get any smaller. If I was ever to move out of right field backup, I had to get better at throwing that damn ball.

Umpire:	Out!
Ruth:	That's three.

The team came jogging in. Sherry and Karen lit cigarettes, Kerry pulled out a fresh bag of spits. A huge bag, a one pounder.

Karen:	Good Lord, there's gotta be enough spitting in that bag to wash a pickup.
Peggy:	I'd say we've got this game in the bag. But the next team we play is supposed to be pretty good.
Debbie:	Yeah, Larry and I are going to check them out.
Sherry:	Why waste your time? Darlene and I are on a roll, right Darlene? We'll just strike 'em all out!
Karen:	Oh Lord, listen to you, I suppose the rest of us should plan on sitting on our arses then, and watch your miraculous performance?

I listened to the banter and braggadocio and wondered if I would get a chance to play at all. The game was close to over, and we had a big lead. Then suddenly, the call came:

Coach:	Michele, after bats, you're in for Debbie, so get ready.

I leapt up, grabbed my glove, asked Debbie to throw a few balls with me to warm up.

The competition was crumbling by then. We maxed out our allowable number of runs per inning. (Such limits come and go from era to era.) We headed out to our positions on the field. I jogged out to right and readied myself for the remote chance a ball would come my way. *Please*, I silently prayed, *send me one fly, just one fly, please!* I wanted to catch a ball, oh how I wanted to feel a ball in my glove! But doubt was still there. Would I lose my grip on the ball? Would I get the ball all the way back to the infield?

Then Debbie was shouting, "MICHELE! BACK UP! SHE CAN GO RIGHT!"

I bolted sideways and began prancing backwards as Sherry sent in the first pitch. The batter let it go.

Umpire: STRRIIKKE!

The batter slowly turned her head and looked at the umpire. Evidently, she didn't agree with the call. The next pitch came fast. Sherry didn't waste time. Again, the batter let it go.

Umpire: STRIIKKE TWO!

This time the batter stepped out of the batter's box, probably rattled now, as she risked being struck out if she did not swing at the next pitch.

With bat already raised she re-entered the batter's box and twisted her front foot into the dirt. Sherry sent her third pitch, high and spinning like a top. The batter shimmied her hips and shook her bat; she was going to go for this pitch, she couldn't afford not to. She lifted her lead leg, I tightened my hand in my glove, tightened my glutes, my calves, my toes. She swung, the bat connected with the ball, the ball was flying up, and up, straight up, I was running in, running, running, but the ball was too far away, I had moved back too far and Kerry had come over from behind second and was standing, waiting for the ball to drop into her glove. SMACK. She had it.

Umpire: OUT!

For the remainder of the game, no other hit went right. My dream of reclaiming past glories would have to wait.

CHAPTER 9

Today, most small Alberta towns with a traffic light have at least one city style café that has nailed cappuccino, morning glory muffins, cream of butternut squash soup, and a micro greens salad. But back in the 80's, small towners had grown up with classic prairie cooking which was known more for its abundance than its gastronomy. Standard summer fare: potato salad smothered in mayo and hard boiled eggs, giant well- done steaks and baked beans. Winter dinners featured pot roasts with frozen peas and corn. Year round, weekend breakfasts were bacon and eggs with white toast.

Naturally, small town restaurant cooks came from these traditions, and since there's comfort in familiarity, they served up their bacon and eggs with McCain's frozen hash browns. McCain's French fries came along with burgers and beef dips too, and there was nothing wrong with serving a beef dip using yesterday's roast beef. A Saturday night steak dinner, however, did call for a little more effort and extravagance. Instead of fries, one could opt for a giant foil- wrapped baked potato heaped with butter AND sour cream AND artificial bacon bits. A steak dinner was always preceded by a special house salad with chunks of iceberg lettuce and a few shreds of carrot and purple cabbage for colour, thoroughly drenched with Kraft Italian dressing. These restaurants did, in the 90's, adopt the more contemporary Caesar salad, putting their own twist on it with Kraft Caesar Dressing and boxed croutons the exact size of mini dice and almost as hard.

While most Rainbows grew up with this culinary experience, I had been fed by a mother whose only bible was the Joy of Cooking. Therefore, I was a food snob. As a teenager, when I wasn't at home eating her perfected version of Manhattan clam chowder or spaghetti bolognese, I was out on dates dining in Calgary's five star steak houses where the garlic toast was made with real French baguettes rather than Wonder Bread. My discriminating taste could detect margarine masquerading as butter and recoiled at the taste of Campbell's chicken noodle soup. I also knew that supermarket deli 'roast turkey' was not actually the meat of a real bird. I did not know what it was, but it was definitely not real turkey.

My uppity palette was revealed to the Rainbows at a local Claresholm diner the first morning of the tournament.

We had arrived at the restaurant and arranged a few arborite topped square tables together. After tucking some folded paper napkins under the legs of the wobbly ones, we settled into our vinyl chairs and began scanning the menu. The waitress poured clay coloured coffee into standard white ceramic mugs.

Trudy:	Geez, you'd think they'd put a little coffee in this water.
Karen:	Good lord, there's not enough caffeine in here to keep a fruit fly awake.

Sonny was pouring sugar into her cup from the dispenser. Scattered around her corner of the table were at least six peeled and emptied little creamers.

Sherry:	Here Sonny, have some more cream, why don'tcha?
Sonny:	Well, I gotta put something in it to make it taste good.

The nearest Rainbows all slid their extra creams over to Sonny, who smirked and continued to peel and pour them into her coffee.

Ruth: There was a really sad story in the news this morning, apparently a woman came into a hospital emergency ward in labour she gave birth and then left, she must have a lot of trouble in her life but still I can't imagine ever leaving one of my girls it's hard to....
Angie: That must be illegal what would you call that anyways?
Kathy: A birth and run?
Debbie: Jesus, Kathy!

The waitress had been taking orders and was now beside me.

Waitress: Can I take your order?
Me: Yes. Do you use real fresh turkey in your clubhouse sandwich?

The waitress seemed flummoxed. I elaborated.

Me: You know, a regular turkey that's been roasted in the oven.
Waitress: Uh, yeah, I think it's been cooked in an oven.

That wasn't the best explanation, I realized.

Me: Sorry, what I mean is, is the turkey that pressed stuff that's made in a factory, or do you guys get a real turkey and roast it here in your own oven. You know, like at Christmas.

The poor girl didn't know what to say.

Me:	Maybe you could check with the chef?
Waitress:	The *chef*? Uh, okay…
Me:	Just ask if the turkey is that rolled pressed stuff or if it's real, ` fresh turkey.

In a daze, the waitress turned away from our table and wandered off, head tilted to one side, as if she was contemplating ancient philosophical questions. I hoped she would just bring out the cook so I could get a straight answer. I was hungry.

I took a sip of my faux coffee and tuned back to the table conversation. Which had died. The team was looking at me. Debbie had a slight smirk on her face, others were trying to stifle laughs.

Karen:	Jesus Christ, the waitress is probably still trying to figure out what the hell you just asked her.
Sherry:	Or maybe she's gone out back to catch a real, fresh, turkey.
Sonny:	I hope not, we'll miss our next game if we have to wait that long.

Being a newbie on a team comprised of people who have worked and played together most of their lives suggests a certain obligation. Like how best to fit in, learn the language of the team. Respect some of the values expressed by the players. In small town southern Alberta this would mean being able to converse about and demonstrate enthusiasm for hockey in general, the local minor team specifically, and all the top players of the NHL. It would also mean talking with keen excitement about the day your own male prodigy will enter the national sport. And finally, it would mean not questioning the origins of the turkey in your clubhouse. I was batting 0 for 3 on all counts.

Despite such a memorable quirk, that night at the big dance, the team forgot about me. I had gone to the ladies room which was some distance across the huge barn like hall where hundreds of locals in wrangler jeans, giant belt buckles and cowboy boots were two stepping through a gorgeous prairie summer night, music blaring, drink and smoke flowing. I returned to our table to find it abandoned. I made my way through the dozens of young farm boys hanging around the exit and out into the parking lot which was filled with trucks. I scanned the parking lot for the Rainbows. Surely, they would be gathered around Kerry's truck waiting for me. Surely.

A couple leaning against a truck making out didn't even register my passing by. The entire town had turned out for the dance, at least two hundred trucks filled the parking lot, but none of them were surrounded by a team of lady ball players. I strolled between the trucks, gravel crunching under my feet, the music in the hall pounding the cool night air. Surely they hadn't left, they must still be here, they must be dancing! Could it be? I hustled back inside. The table was empty, but the dance floor was packed. I walked around the perimeter, then weaved my way through the dancers. No Rainbows.

Reluctantly I concluded, the Rainbows had left.

It must have been the turkey. They just didn't understand about the turkey.

I plowed through the farm boys at the door and found the pay phone. Fortunately, Claresholm was big enough to support a single taxi. Within two minutes of placing the call, I was in the front seat telling the driver to start heading south.

Me:	I don't have an address, I've only been to the house once, but if you start driving around on the south side of town I'll see it sooner or later.

The driver looked at me for a very long ten seconds. I could see he was trying to decide if this was going to be worth his while or not.

Me:	Don't worry, I'll pay you whatever it costs.
Driver:	Okay lady.

In anxious silence I rode in the cab from the door of the hall to the end of the parking lot, at which point a suburban came flying at us, causing the cab driver to yank the wheel to the right to avoid a collision. Kerry was waving her arm out the driver's window and Debbie had leaped out of the passenger side and run to the cab to retrieve me.

I got in the truck.

Kerry:	Michele, I'm so sorry! I can't believe we left without you. You must have felt awful.
Debbie:	I thought Trudy had her eye on you, but apparently she thought the same thing about me. Jesus Christ, I'm just glad we noticed you were missing before we all went to bed!

I'm not sure how much abuse rookies should have to tolerate, but I was too relieved to care. The team seemed to be particularly sensitive to my whereabouts for the rest of the weekend, and not a word was said about my turkey, which by the way, was indeed, fake meat.

WHEN I ARRIVED HOME EARLY SUNDAY EVENING, I FOUND MY TWO precious sons in the living room, gloriously naked but for diapers, crawling and drooling over the toy-strewn carpet and Husband, who looked like he had been rushed and crushed by an entire NHL team.

I threw myself down on the floor and took my boys into a bear hug and felt my love for them surge through and over me like a tsunami. They hadn't drowned in the dugout. They hadn't morphed into emaciated waifs. They were happy to see me but were happy without me. Husband had not hired a live in replacement caregiver. While away *doing something for myself,* my real world had remained intact.

CHAPTER 10

Having married at age 20, I had few peers to refer to when assessing the quality of my marriage. Nor could I measure progress against any maternal advice or wisdom; my mother had married at age 16 and so, when I announced to her with absurd confidence that I was going to marry and have a baby, she only nodded and said something like, 'how wonderful'.

I entered the state of matrimony thrilled to be pregnant and certain I would reach the silver, gold, and platinum years in a state of enviable bliss. My commitment to this long game was still unwavering when I joined the Rainbows, but I had begun to understand that the bliss part was not guaranteed. Bliss, I was learning, was really not the correct adjective to aim for when working on a marriage. Bloodless, I think now, is more realistic. Followed by placatory.

As my first season with the Rainbows unfolded and I got to know my teammates, I began to see that marriage could function under a broad spectrum of conditions. Almost every one of the Rainbows at that time were married, but they did not all follow the same rules, and most of them were certainly not following mine. While I marched to Guilt's drum as I prepared for my once a week outing with the Rainbows, many of them were joining mixed slo-pitch leagues and golf leagues, and had already signed up for the winter curling season. And I was certain none of them bothered to run these plans by their spouses. As far as I could tell, these women, with their careers and their recreational activities, did not lay awake at night trying to devise solutions to intractable marital problems. It became apparent to me that they expected intractable marital problems and knew the best response was to give equal weight to their own individual fulfillment. Somehow, despite my certainty that I knew everything I needed to know, I had missed that lesson.

This sense of independence explains why the state of our collective marriages was not a Rainbows topic of discussion. At the pub after games, we thoroughly analyzed all seven innings, cracked up over outrageous plays, and told jokes. If anyone's marriage was in trouble, it was never put on the table. It would have spoiled our fun.

As things turned out, six of us ended up divorced. Sherry was the first.

In 1980, eyebrows were still being raised when women took the divorce plunge. But for Sherry, who had two small children at the time, social trends and social approval were irrelevant; she would have divorced and gone off to raise her two kids on her own even if she had been living in Victorian England. A bookkeeper by day and a free soul by night, Sherry simply couldn't care less. She brought home the bacon, put her son through hockey and her daughter through volleyball and ball, and liked the colour of her hair. She had a house, she had a car, she had a good mother, and a good father too, she had a friend who loved her….Sherry probably didn't like that Jann Arden Song, too sappy, she would say, but she would know the words and could sing it if you asked her. And really, she lived the song. She did like the colour of her hair, a nice coppery blond, she always had money in her pocket (but not necessarily in the bank), and she always, always, faced forward by herself. Sherry was the embodiment of the liberated woman. By the time she settled on another man her two children were well into their teens and, aside from having to deal with lupus, she had not a care in the world. Lupus is an autoimmune disease, which means the body produces antibodies whether you need them or not. These hyper antibodies attack the body's own tissues. Treatment can include immuno-suppressive drugs and all lupus victims are advised to avoid the sun between 10 a.m. and 4 p.m. Sherry played ball and golfed at high noon and didn't give a damn. She didn't need the drugs because she suppressed her own immune system with a couple of bad habits. This was her theory anyway, and it worked long enough for her to put in a few decades on the ball fields and golf links around southern Alberta and become a grandma.

The new man she eventually chose was not only athletic like Sherry but also ten years her junior, officially making Sherry the cougar in our pack. Her new man understood Sherry could play any sport and drink as many beers as he could so they would have to take turns being the driver when they were at a tournament together. He may have been a country boy, but clearly, he was a liberated one.

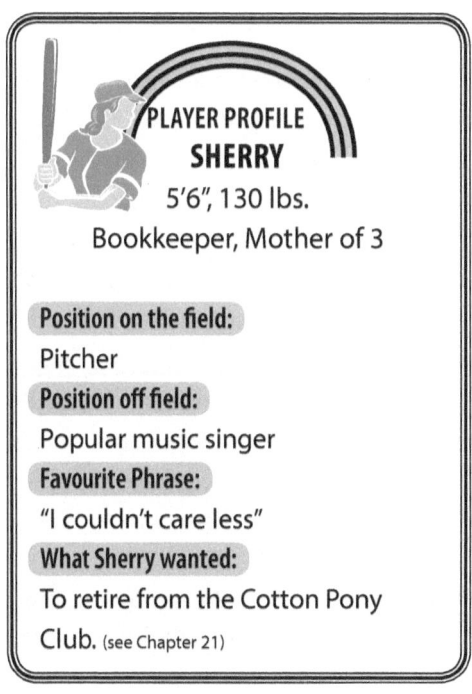

PLAYER PROFILE
SHERRY
5'6", 130 lbs.
Bookkeeper, Mother of 3

Position on the field:
Pitcher
Position off field:
Popular music singer
Favourite Phrase:
"I couldn't care less"
What Sherry wanted:
To retire from the Cotton Pony Club. (see Chapter 21)

Sherry was a talented and fearless pitcher. Before taking her position in the infield, she would load the back pocket of her ball pants with spits and then kind of stroll to her position and casually toss two or three practice pitches before the first batter entered the box. Then, her hand would go into her back pocket and come out with a palm full of seeds which would all go in her mouth at once. This was an extraordinary feat – the oral manipulation of 20 or so spits at once, while pitching.

This skill and habit with sunflower seeds was the equivalent of the American baseball player who chewed tobacco while leaping into the air to snag a fly ball before it went into the stands, but without the side effects of brown teeth, rotten breath, and a frightful tumour- like wad pressing against the inside of the cheek. Sherry had nice teeth and liked to smile.

She also liked to smoke and drink and sing and sometimes pull down strings of patio lanterns in pubs when she was Standing Inside the Fire with Garth Brooks, or she was feeling like one of those Girls who Just Wanna Have Fun. She was a country, pop, and rock lyrics encyclopedia with an alto voice that would have been the perfect counterpoint and drinking buddy for Janis Joplin. Not only would Sherry have kept up with Janis, she would have given her a few pointers in the man department too.

Batting and running the bases were activities equally incidental to her favourite pursuits and rarely did she allow these aspects of her sport to interfere with her habits. If she decided during a game that she wanted a smoke, which she frequently did, she would light up and puff away until five seconds before she was due in the batter's box. She would then pass the lit cigarette to the nearest fellow smoker with one of two possible requests. 'Put it out', meant it was worth saving, and 'smoke it if you want', meant it wasn't.

As irreverent as Sherry was, she recognized her limits. She never mixed her paralyzers with her beer.

Sonny was just 18 when she became a Rainbow. Despite coming from a strict Mormon family, she fit nicely with the Rainbows approach to leisure time. Had her family known the Rainbows were in their daughter's future, they might have placed her in a Catholic convent to save her from her own destiny, but fortunately, she was free to embrace her official adult status surrounded by women who understood her need to cut loose now and then.

Sonny seemed to me to be in the midst of great change, change in line with a progressive society but I, with my two children, Husband, mortgage, and ideals, viewed her as if from a different planet. The fact that we were only five years apart in age did not help me bridge the gap, but rather, reinforced the fact that it is not age, but experience, that separates us.

Had I taken a cue from Sonny, I might have recognized a need for more remedial play in my life. When I was 18, instead of joining in on as many sports as possible and howling at the moon as she was, I was working full time, supporting myself, and taking every opportunity that came my way to enlighten friends and family about the dangers in the world. Dangers like world religions, dictators, nuclear power, and Amway. I was, at age 18, an annoyingly righteous know-it-all.

Sonny was quick to discover the Rainbows pot of gold was filled with all the things her heart desired, which happened to be all the things her Mormon upbringing forbade. Although beer and cigarettes figured prominently in the material items, they were really for Sonny more of a conduit to the freedom she sought from the Mormon proscription of how a young lady should behave. Sonny didn't care for makeup, dresses and cute sandals, she preferred pants and loafers. She wasn't interested in the domestic skill sets promoted for Mormon women. Cooking, cleaning, sewing and gardening would have interfered with her sports schedule, which was packed, since she was a natural athlete. She played on several ball teams and golfed all spring, summer, and fall, then played basketball all winter. Apparently she worked as well, but I never heard her talk much about her job. She wasn't a career girl; she was still trying to please her Mormon family so she got married when she was 20. As we were all unsanctified apostates, the Rainbows were invited only to the post ceremony celebration which took place in the gymnasium and involved tippling lemonade and nibbling on crust less sandwiches. As far as I know, no one snuck in a mickey of vodka with which to spike the virgin beverage, but I know it was on the minds of some.

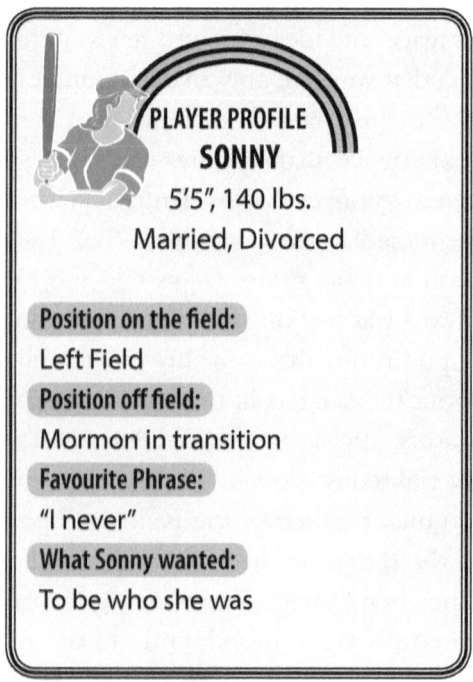

Everyone, including Sonny, was surprised to see her in a white wedding dress, but as I recall the dress was the only concession she made to tradition, aside from the marriage itself. Her long brown wavy hair remained down and unadorned, her face free of cosmetics, and her feet free of heels. Her husband was kind and gentle and when they divorced a year later continued to be a friend to Sonny and the Rainbows.

Sonny moved to Calgary but continued on the Rainbows for a few more years, knocking the ball out of the park every time she was up to bat. Left field was her domain. She roamed it like a well fed lioness that was only hunting for fun, never missing her prey. Everyone on the bench respected this youngest member of the team for her athletic superiority and was grateful for her participation, since she was our ace, but no one aside from perhaps Sherry, really knew her. She was something of a mystery to us and perhaps she was to herself as well at that time in her life. I imagine transitioning from a strict church to a loose secular based life was full of surprises and confusions.

ANGIE WAS NOT ONE TO BE OVERLOOKED. A SUITABLE METAPHOR for Angie's essential character, as, on most days, she was hard to miss and if it looked like she was going to be missed, she would make some kind of play to make sure she wasn't. This comes naturally to anyone who is or should have been a performer. Since Angie was in sales most of her life, she was a sort of performer and I learned in my first year with the Rainbows that she was going to be a prime source of entertainment.

I liked to sit near Angie at the pub after games so I could listen to her mangle the English language in her rush to get out all the impressions and thoughts flitting in and out of her mind, many of which were based on newspaper articles she had read while gobbling down her pork chops and mashed potatoes before the game.

Angie was the first Rainbow to appear in spandex. This would have been around 1986, so her spandex was first generation, meaning it was not tempered, as stretch pants are today, with a little relaxation. These babies clung to her voluptuous thighs and middle the way static charged plastic wrap clings to your hand when you want it to cling to a bowl of leftovers. Furthermore, her spandex pants were enhanced with the name of an Australian beer, Fosters, emblazoned in giant letters down one of those thighs. Foster's had recently been acquired in Canada by her employer, Molson's, a company for which Angie was the ideal representative, since beer was her beverage of choice. With the advertising and the extraordinary appearance of her lower half encased in this new fabric, her electric blue eyeshadow and black eyeliner, top and bottom, her Parade Pink lipstick, and auburn hair, Angie stood out. So did her honest commentary, which was a feature film that anyone was welcome to attend for free. Example – at the pub after a game: '

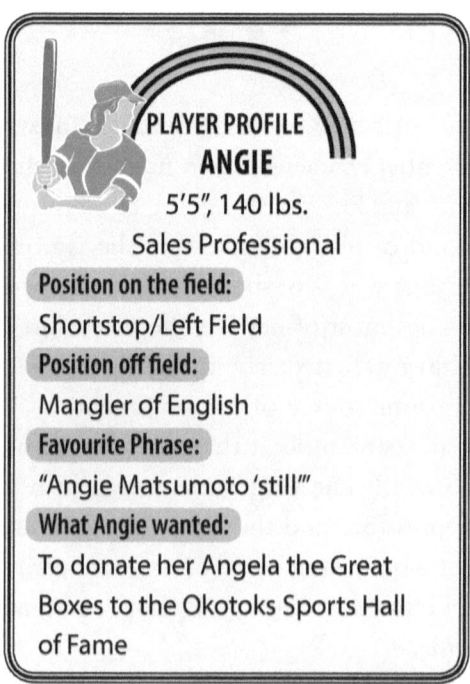

PLAYER PROFILE
ANGIE
5'5", 140 lbs.
Sales Professional
Position on the field:
Shortstop/Left Field
Position off field:
Mangler of English
Favourite Phrase:
"Angie Matsumoto 'still'"
What Angie wanted:
To donate her Angela the Great Boxes to the Okotoks Sports Hall of Fame

Angie: Did you get a load of those girls? Christ, their boobs were bigger than my thighs and that's saying a lot since as you know I've got a pair of thunder thighs, even though I lost five pounds this winter. Can you tell? Please tell me you can tell, even if you can't, it was shittin' hard to lose them. I only drank one beer on curling nights and didn't eat a single chicken wing for a month'.

While Angie takes a breath Kathy slides in a shot:

Kathy: Jesus Angie, quit your whining, wouldja?

to which Angie replies,

Angie: Easy for you to say Atkins, you can drink and eat as much as you want and still be skinny as a tree. Wait a minute, trees aren't really skinny are they. Skinny as a skinny tree. Oh poo-poo, forget it, you know what I mean. One of these days Atkins, you're gonna have a cougar belly, believe me, there's no getting' out of it. Hey, did anyone see Rob? I thought him and Brian would come over for a beer.

The two men, one husband and one live in, had sat in Brian's pickup watching the game.

Angie: They're probably still sitting in Brian's truck drinking beer, damn it. I want to make sure Rob didn't miss my homer.

Debbie: Oh for chrissakes, it's not like he hasn't seen that before!

Kathy: You're as blind as a bat Matsumoto. The guys have been sitting over there since we came in.

Angie pulls off her glasses, squints into the corner of the bar and sees Brian, legs and body stretched out in a chair, arm resting on table, hand around beer mug. Across from him is Rob, back to all of us, hunched over the table facing Brian.

Angie: Rooooobbb! Rob darling, what are you doing over there?

Rob cranks his neck over his shoulder and glances at our table, turns back and continues his conversation with Brian.

Angie: Roobbb! Did you see my home run?

Rob waves his hand but doesn't turn around.

Angie: Well, shit, would you look at that, how rude! I'm gonna have to have a talk with him later, damn it, I don't like it when he doesn't answer me. Does your husband do that?
Kathy: He's not your husband Angie.
Angie: I know! God damn it that's another thing that really bugs me!

Angie's last name from her first marriage was Matsumoto but she had been waiting a very long time to change it to Wedderburn. This explains why one of her favourite refrains was, "Hi, I'm Angie Matsumoto. Still."

CHAPTER 11

CIGARETTE SMOKE CLUNG TO THE CEILING OF THE BASEMENT BANquet room of the Okotoks Masonic Hall. The Rainbows and their spouses and friends had just finished the Lazy L's catered roast beef dinner. Lester himself was there, overseeing things. Dishes clanged in the kitchen, and chatter reverberated off the plywood lined walls and thin wooden chairs. The Masonic Hall was a cheap rental which suited our team budget very well.

It was November, harvest was over, and the time had arrived for each Rainbow to be teased, poked, or humiliated at the annual Rainbows Wind Up Banquet and Roast, an event that, by the end of the night, I figured would have made even Martin and Sinatra blush.

At my table I sat with Husband and other Rainbows and their spouses, soaking up this end of season social with a bloody caesar and a cigarette. I couldn't believe my luck. Rarely did I go to banquets with a catered dinner and a program. It may not have been a five star event at a golf and country club, but at this event, we were the stars of our own show and I was about to be roasted for the very first time. This was something new and different, and I was always game for new and different.

The music stopped and Debbie was tapping on the microphone.

Debbie: Let's begin the festivities, shall we?

She had a glint her eye as she launched into the first award.

Debbie:	Peggy is our team sergeant. She makes sure we stay on the straight and narrow during games. Well, she tries anyway…

After recounting Peggy's objections to a couple of benched players cracking open a beer during a game, Peggy was presented with the Colonel Klink award, and was photographed standing before the audience wearing a copy of the Commandant's cap.

Karen received The Best Snatch Award in recognition of an extraordinary catch she had made at third during a league game. The line drive went right off the bat and into a mysterious invisible glove wedged between her upper thighs, where it remained until the umpire yelled 'OUT!'

This was followed by Darlene, who was gifted with a handmade matching set of earrings and necklace, made of delicately strung and suspended tampons, died Rainbow kelly green, naturally, to remind her that being unprepared is no excuse for abandoning the pitchers position in the middle of a game.

In horror I watched as Rainbow after Rainbow was dragged before the audience and skewered. I sipped my caesar and racked my brain. What humiliation was I about to endure? Reflecting on the summer, aside from my trouble getting a proper grip on the melon ball, I thought I had conducted myself fairly well. No obvious misdeed came to mind, yet I knew I was in for something special, because my award had been saved for last.

I watched Debbie and Kerry speak quietly to each other and then Kerry zipped up the stairs next to the stage and disappeared through a dark recess. Debbie tapped on the microphone and the audience quieted.

Debbie:	And now, last but far from least, our newest player, Michele. We welcomed Michele to the Rainbows back in April when she called Trudy looking for a team to join. We

needed a new recruit so we invited her out to a practice. She looked pretty good so we decided to invite her to join the team and I think it was a good decision. She acquitted herself well throughout the season. Once she got the hang of the pitch, she made a few good hits and out in field she didn't let any balls by her. At our Claresholm tournament in July, we found out that not only had we picked up a decent ball player, but also an admirer of gourmet food. We learned that Michele has very particular tastes. For example, did you know, that the turkey in clubhouse sandwiches is not always real? Apparently, it's often made in a factory with fake turkey. This revelation was revealed to us during a post-game brunch when Michele, who was hankering for a clubhouse, asked the waitress if the turkey was real. 'Is it real, fresh, turkey', she said, 'or is it that fake, pressed stuff from the factory?' The poor waitress had no idea what she was talking about. And neither did we. Michele asked the waitress, very politely I might add, to please check with the cook. Actually, she said chef. Well, as it turned out, the turkey they used in their clubhouses was not the real, fresh stuff Michele wanted. She was clearly very disappointed and so, we are hoping our gift to you Michele, will lift your spirits.

A door squeaked open, a puff of cold air descended into the room, and out of the dark recess came Kerry with her husband

Jack, maneuvering a large sheet draped object down the stairs. My fear grew as they crossed the front of the room and carefully placed the object on the table. The crowd tittered and giggled as I obeyed Debbie's command to come to the front. With a signal from Debbie, Kerry and Jack lifted the sheet, revealing a large cage inside of which strutted a real, fresh, live.... chicken. Apparently, there were no turkeys available. They had all been slaughtered for Thanksgiving.

When the laughter died down the music came on and for the rest of the night my chicken and I danced to the alternating sounds of the likes of Rodney Crowell and John Mellencamp.

Since I had not come to the party with the chicken, at the end of the night I felt no obligation to go home with it either. I gave the bird to Kerry, thanked her for taking it off my hands, and went home with a sense of relief.

Had I known that evening that I would soon become a chicken farmer, I might have arranged room and board for my award until my own barn was fitted up with a waterer, feeder, and straw. However, like so many other choices I have made, I had little advance warning I was going to make this one.

CHAPTER 12

WHILE THE RAINBOWS HAD REAWAKENED MY PRE-MOTHERHOOD identity and rescued me from drowning in my own dugout of conscientiousness and do-gooding, I wasn't about to become a complete convert to carefree, guilt free living. Outside of my weekly four hour time out with the Rainbows, I took my personal growth and parenting responsibilities very seriously. To ease my young son's eczema, I began sourcing pure cotton fabrics (the '80's was the decade of better than the '70's polyester) and picked up old sewing patterns to have his clothes tailor made. I travelled far and wide to purchase organic yogourt. I grew that huge garden which required hours of back breaking weeding, picking, and processing. And, to better myself intellectually and prepare for that day when I would pursue a real career, I entered long distance university.

I also began raising my own hormone and antibiotic free, free range chickens. I embarked on this endeavor after tasting a neighbour's home grown chicken. The bird had been raised on the land, where it pecked at a variety of plants such as chickweed, dandelion, and clover, all of which also grew in abundance around my barn and none of which was ever sprayed with anything other than deer and bunny pee and sometimes little boy pee. The chicken also tasted transcendental.

Debbie couldn't understand why I wanted to raise my own chickens. After a game one night:

Debbie:	I'll head down to the Lazy L and get us a table.
Me:	Don't worry about saving me a spot tonight Debbie.
Debbie:	Why not?
Me:	I have to go home and check on my chicks.
Debbie:	What? What are you doing now? You mean baby chickens?
Me:	Yeah, those.
Debbie:	What the hell are you doing with baby chickens?
Me:	I've decided to raise my own chicken. I don't like all that stuff they put in store bought chickens.
Debbie:	What stuff?
Me:	You know, antibiotics and growth hormones and everything. Plus, they inject water into the chickens to make them seem juicy. Did you know that?
Debbie:	Whatever. I've never had a problem with chicken. How many do you have?
Me:	Just 25.
Debbie:	So you're going to raise chickens now. As if you don't have enough to do already. You're nuts.

Raising chickens requires daily attendance to their needs. And a nose plug. They begin as cute little balls of yellow fluff that need nothing more than a straw filled box and a heat lamp. During this stage my little boys and I visited the chicks dozens of times a day, making sure their water and food dispensers were full and cuddling each one of them at least once during every visit. This cute and vulnerable stage lasts no more than a week, after which they rapidly transform into squawking, smelling, nonstop poopers that can never get enough food and do not mind sleeping in their own excrement. We stopped holding them and began herding them out of the barn and into their outdoor pecking run which we had created with chicken wire and posts. While they foraged on weeds and grass outside, I replaced the poop saturated straw inside with fresh straw. My chicken farming attire included black rubber boots, plain canvas gardening gloves, and a pitchfork. Those home grown chickens were delicious, juicy and meaty and full of flavour, and they produced gravy that would make an Alabama granny blush with pride. But getting them to the freezer was a gruesome business that, fortunately, the local Hutterites were more than happy to handle.

The farm to plate odyssey began with a pre-dawn round-up. Capturing twenty-five full grown, flighty and suspicious chickens is a traumatic experience. And I don't mean for the birds. Sneaking into the barn under cover of darkness when the birds are roosting, feels underhanded enough, but when the birds awaken to the fact that they are being captured they become frantic. Telling them there is nothing to be frightened of, they are just going for a ride and there will be snacks, does not help. They do not want to leave their barn and they will flap their wings and run and squawk until every last one is settled in the cage in the back of the pickup. Once together again, they are content and probably asking each other what all the fuss was about.

The drive down highway 2 to the nearest Hutterite Colony took an hour, but the birds were quiet and so was I, as the sunrise over the prairie is a spectacular sight that gives one a feeling of destiny. Surely, if such heavenly beauty accompanied our trip to meet our maker, the journey was written long ago.

Raising your own chickens and then taking them to be butchered at a Hutterite colony is something every Canadian should experience at least once. Witnessing the process is educational, the Hutterites allow you to follow along as the animals are killed, de-feathered, eviscerated, inspected, and freezer bagged. This may sound unpleasant, and it is, but with the experience also comes a spiritual awakening.

Chickens ask nothing more of life than to be left alone to eat and peck and cluck and roost. They are being prepared to feed people, and the chickens themselves seem to know they are being prepared to feed people, because they do nothing more than eat and sleep, thereby fattening themselves. When you are face to face with this reality, standing in your rubber boots atop the poopy straw in your barn, and then standing next to your caged birds as they await their turn with the Hutterite named Dave at the chopping block, you feel great gratitude. Gratitude and awe. How is it that this earth is such a cornucopia of food fit for humans? How is it that we can live peacefully with the animals that feed us? For eons human beings have been raising animals for consumption, yet these animals have not genetically adapted to this fact by evolving an Escape Gene. Century after century, they continue to live with us, sustaining us with their milk, their feathers and wool, and their flesh. Witnessing the life and death of these animals, one cannot help but be awakened.

At the pub on game nights, I didn't share my awakening with the Rainbows. They would have been convinced that I was a little loopy. Plus, I might have spoiled their enjoyment of our platter of ten cent chicken wings. And make no mistake, after a game, Canada's recreational slo-pitch players love to down dozens and dozens of wings with their beers.

CHAPTER 13

Winter descended on the post ball season world. Life looked like this:

Outside, the cold north wind ripped the frozen earth from its hiding place under the barley field stubble and flung it across the driveway upon which my eyes were trained daily at 4:00 p.m. in anticipation of Husband's return and my subsequent salvation. In winter we became a two parent household, as Husband could not stop the sky from darkening at 5:00 p.m. nor thaw the frozen earth.

Standing at the window with my boys at my feet, I would watch them and will the peace to last until Husband returned. My oldest, now a reasonably self-controlled three and a half year old, would be constructing bridges with his Duplo. My youngest, taking cues from his brother, would be laying out roads with the red Duplo his brother had generously allowed him. Peaceful and quiet.

But soon, it would be, as my Mother's Almanac so aptly named it, Arsenic Hour. The youngest would eye his brother's bridges and decide they needed to be deconstructed. The bridge builder would passively resist this attack on his creation for a surprisingly long time, perhaps five whole minutes, before silently expressing his frustration by pushing his brother over and escaping to a far corner of the room, taking back all the red Duplo.

Willing the peace and quiet to continue. Knowing it would not. Watching for Husband. Thinking of the work ahead that night, in the cold basement office to which I would retreat to work on my first university course. *Do something for yourself* had awakened not only my pre-motherhood identity as a ball player, but also one of my life long dreams of obtaining a university education. I wanted a *real* career when my children grew up. I wanted to *be somebody*. All of the Rainbows had careers, some were professionals. They had gone to university before they had their children. I would have to do that while I raised mine. I had discovered long distance university and enrolled in my first course. Child Psychology.

I used my sons as subjects for my assignments. Pre-Arsenic Hour, I would drop to the floor and enter their playground. Soon, both sons would abandon their Duplo and dig out their bulldozers and graders from the toy box. My body would become the construction site as one steered his bulldozer carefully up my leg (imagining, I assumed, the stubble on my leg was a forest that needed dozing), while the other plowed his roller through my cleavage. I would make mental notes of their behaviour. They did not speak to each other while they played. They would accommodate each other's space, but if one invaded the others', there would be a non-verbal response. A slight adjustment to maintain the prescribed distance. A turned back. A toy grab. This last one having the potential to escalate into an all-out toy war.

Recognizing the signs of the coming breakdown, I would suggest we read a Beatrix Potter.

Beatrix Potter stories fascinated my sons. Long, thoughtful sagas, accompanied by wee little sketches in watery pastel colours with fine lines that disappeared into the creamy nether world of rabbit holes and garden sheds and impossibly cozy mice retreats.

Ben:	Why did Mr. MacGregor put all the rabbits in the bag?
Josh:	Cuz he's gonna kill them!
Ben:	Why?
Josh:	Cuz they ate his lettuce!

Ben: Is he right Mommy?

It was true, life in the country could be nasty and mean with stinging wasps and biting red ants and stinking skunks that had to be neutralized. But life in the country could also be magical, filled with butterflies, birds and pop up gophers. And cute little rabbits. I liked rabbits. Rabbits could eat their fill of my garden lettuce. Rabbits were in my magic category. And therefore, Josh's bullseye shocked me. How did he know what Mr. MacGregor was going to do?

Me: No, he's just going to drive them somewhere far away from his garden and let them go.
Josh: No he's not! He's going to kill them! He's going to drown them in the pond!

Ben looked at his brother. He looked at me. Then he slid off the sofa and went to build Duplo bridges.

The block building would suffice for perhaps ten or fifteen more minutes, and then, they would begin to Fuss.

They would begin to Fuss and they would continue to Fuss through the following attempts at stopping the Fussing:

Cuddles and Tickles and Kisses.

Watching the Ball Go Down the Stairs.

Snacks.

Helping Mommy Dial Daddy's Phone Number. Wait, that's not possible; cell phones weren't invented yet. I must have been dreaming. Wow, I could have invented cell phones if only I didn't have to deal with fussy children.

And this would just be Monday.

Despite the anticipation of my evenings of university work, the winter days dragged. My once a week reprieve, a morning spent in the nearby DeWinton Community Hall basement with

25 other fussing giggling running preschoolers and their mothers wasn't until Wednesday, which by 4:00 p.m. Monday, felt about as far off as one of my other dreams – a round trip walking tour of planet Earth.

Although there are immeasurable doses of profound joy in being our children's primary caregiver, one morning per week at the playschool was not sufficient to satisfy my need for adult company. I considered a part time job, but I did not feel my preschoolers were ready yet, or perhaps, I wasn't ready yet, to leave their regular care up to a babysitter.

Struggling with this dilemma had become a daily challenge when, one morning while watching Sesame Street and spooning Pedialyte into the mouths of my sons both of whom were down with gastroenteritis, an ad appeared on television. A local boarding school for emotionally disturbed teenagers was seeking volunteers, people who would come and spend a few hours a week in a classroom to help the regular teacher and provide some enrichment within the program. These kids needed mentors, big brothers and sisters, people who were not there to teach them the daily rules of living and learning, but rather, could just chow down with them during snack breaks and maybe help them figure out how to use a computer, which had recently been introduced to the world. Well, I could do the snack thing, I thought. Computers were yet to enter my universe.

Yes, I know. Saner mothers with no budget to work with would have taken an afternoon a week to wander around a mall, go visit a friend, or read a book and nap.

But when the brief advertisement ended I discovered tears had sprung from my eyes. I felt as though a hand had reached out from the television and into my body and yanked on my heart and my soul.

> Josh: Why are you crying Mommy?
> Me: Oh, because I just love you sooooo much!

Ben: But why does that make you cry?
Me: Because I feel sooooo lucky to be your mommy that it makes me cry happy tears! Let's read a Beatrix Potter!

Later, I called the home and offered myself as a volunteer. My sense that I was doing the right thing was unequivocal, and when I hung up the phone my emotions had calmed and I felt a powerful new sense of purpose. And I utterly failed to recognize that the commitment would not bring into my life the adult company I was craving.

That night, after the routine of dinnertime, bathtime, storytime (*I Love You Forever*, *Goodnight Moon*), and bedtime dispelled Potter's gruesome life lessons, I changed into my ugly furry brown outfit in preparation for my evening study in the meat cooler.

On my way down the hall I passed Josh's room. Hearing him whimper, I gently pushed open the creaky door and slipped in, tiptoed to his child- size bed and examined him for vital signs. He was warm in his pure cotton pajamas which had not eased his eczema, his Sesame Street Big Bird blanket rose and fell with his breathing which just then was deep. I waited for him to settle, wondered if I should give him a kiss, if this would wake him or comfort him. He hadn't been feeling quite right, a cough had been nagging him, but, with no other symptoms I expected it to go away on its own.

I stood with my hand lightly resting on this son's back, watching and feeling him go deeper into sleep, feeling my love enter his body, imagining it as an elixir, a dose of pure, magic, medicine. Reluctantly, I stole out of his room, feeling I was stealing my love from him by leaving him, but there was this other self that must also be obeyed.

As I descended the stairs that evening, I thought of the tears that came to my eyes, the twist I felt in my stomach, the ache I felt in my heart, when I heard the call for volunteers for those children.

Why did I have such a powerful response? It had taken me completely by surprise. At that moment, in the presence of my children, I could only take a deep breath and push away the images that had rushed into my mind like wind through a tunnel. And just like wind that enters a tunnel furiously and then settles into a calmer presence, the images slowed, and then hovered, in a dark, blatant, silence. Irrevocably there. Images of the children of a remote village in Canada's north. A dysfunctional village I had lived in briefly as a child. Images of small crying children, images of older children, my friends, who, like me, knew there was a bigger brighter world beyond the bush shrouded village through which we roamed together, from river to ravine to rundown hotel. Until, one day, abruptly, with my family, I left. And, like a survivor of a tragedy, had never forgotten.

I didn't understand then, that my visceral response to that ad was guilt, and the sense of purpose I felt when I volunteered was my way of atoning for leaving my friends, for getting out of that village while they remained. If I couldn't help them, I could help others.

On my drive home from my volunteer interview I felt shaken. I was entering a world of harmed and hurting children who needed the steady hand and heart of their teachers and volunteers like me. My role would be to support a teacher of a class of upper elementary aged kids with a variety of emotional and behavioural challenges. I would read to them in small groups, have snack time with them, be a helping hand. Was I up to it? I was just 23 years old, what could I offer?

I found out quickly that my presence and my desire to ease the day for these kids in whatever way I could, was more than enough. I was another adult with a calm voice giving complete attention to their needs.

As the weekly volunteer afternoons added up, I felt my sense of worth increase. Just as so many others before me have learned, in helping others there is a sense that we receive far more than we give.

Which is why I felt so bad when, on my third year of volunteering, I scared the daylights out of the kids when I appeared in a mask for Halloween. I didn't think it was a scary mask, it was just the rubber face of an old man with a big goofy grin. To completely disguise myself, I borrowed my mother's ankle length leather and fur winter coat. Apparently, troubled kids do not appreciate this kind of deception.

That first winter between ball seasons was one of profound self-discovery. But when spring came and I got out on the field again with the Rainbows and my old ball glove, a remnant of my time in the north, I didn't mention to these new friends the history of that glove, or my volunteering. I just entered the circle of friendship, with gratitude, and with hope.

CHAPTER 14

BALL SEASON WAS COMING UP AND I KNEW IF THERE WAS ANY HOPE for me to move into the infield, I would need a new glove. Giving up an old glove is not an easy thing. Ball players get attached to their gloves the way toddlers get attached to stuffies. The ball glove, or mitt, is the only piece of equipment in which an amateur player really needs to invest. Cleats, those shoes with spikes on the bottom, are nice, but not essential for the recreational slo-pitch player. A pair of cross trainers with deep treads work well enough in normal conditions, and if it's down to a choice between spending money on a pair of cleats or say, a Mother's Day gift, Mom should win the day.

But the choice of ball glove cannot be sacrificed for Mom. This essential item is crucial to a player's performance and therefore must be chosen with great care. Once a new glove is selected and purchased, it is put through weeks and sometimes months of trials before a final decision is made on its worthiness.

A good glove slides onto the hand, well, like a glove, allowing ease of entry and exit. Once on, the palm of the hand must stick to the glove while allowing the fingers to move inside their respective cavities.

The combination of palm immobility and finger mobility is critical because a hard hit ball will knock an ill-fitting glove right off the player's hand.

A good glove maintains the round cavity where the ball is caught, but at the same time softens so the fingers of the glove become flat and open and close like a door. To achieve this condition most players will try to work the stiffness away by sitting on the glove, or pounding on it in their spare time. The glove is abandoned if it doesn't cooperate, and the player goes back to her old worn out duct taped glove until she can get to the nearest Sport Chek and try again.

After multiple visits to the sports store and hours of agonizing, I settled on a medium brown Wilson. Nothing wrong with its appearance but it could never compare to the beauty of my old glove which I found in 1974 in a dark corner of a wooden shelf loaded with thermal underwear, in the Watson Lake, Yukon, General Store. That was a beautiful, beautiful glove. The fingers alternated in colour, dark chocolate brown against light tan. Colours like the best looking thoroughbreds at the track. Rich leather scent. Beautiful. There was nothing like it, anywhere. It cost $70, which was a fortune for a glove in 1974. My new glove cost about the same, in 1986.

The new Wilson passed the probation period, but it took me a couple of seasons to completely switch my allegiance from my old glove to this new one. People like Rumi and Buddha and probably Dr. Seuss say we should never get attached to things, that attachment is self-imprisonment. Being tied to the physical world is like chaining ourselves to a place or to things, thereby making it impossible for our minds and souls to travel to other realms, to other levels of consciousness, where great wisdom awaits us.

However, certain physical objects can become a portal to those places. My old glove is still with me, and sometimes I touch it as I squeeze past where it rests on a shelf in my garage, in order to get into my old truck that has well over 200,000 km on it. So far.

KATHY EPITOMIZED BALL GLOVE ATTACHMENT. SHE LOATHED THE idea of replacing it but when the duct tape started to unravel, she embarked on her hunt for a new one. Since we are both lefties, one of the first things she did when she met me was to check out my glove. When she gave it her approval, I felt I had passed the Kathy test.

Kathy was a star shortstop who carried her ball glove around with the attention and care one carries a newborn. However, her glove was ancient, so worn it flapped in a strong wind. Kathy was also a cynic. Cynical characters are prime opportunities for writers to create narrative tension, because cynicism can serve as a disguise for genuine moral corruption, or in the least, an excuse for never making charitable donations. Fortunately for the Rainbows and the world, Kathy's cynicism was only a disguise for a gigantic soft spot. She talked a tough talk but get her around babies, kids, or innocent animals and her tough talk transformed into granny like croons.

Kathy became a Rainbow after leaving the DeWinton Diggers because she was tired of losing games to the Rainbows. Whether she was poached by Debbie or came to us as a defector of her own accord remains a closely guarded secret. Unlike most other players such as me, Kathy did not have to work her way up the ranks from catcher or right to a position with more star quality. Since she had already proven herself in the league as a top player, she was immediately given the position of shortstop. Thereby bumping Angie, who had coveted shortstop the way one covets things like brand new sports cars, or standing invitations to private boxes at professional sports stadiums.

When Debbie delicately explained to Angie that this change was going to occur and, since Sonny had left, Angie would now be the Rainbows left fielder, Angie wouldn't admit it, but she was pissed.

Debbie:	So you're okay with going to left? We need you out there now that Sonny's leaving.
Angie:	I guess since Atkins can't run she has to have an infield position. Not everyone can

play equally well in the outfield and the infield, so I guess I should be flattered. Left field's a tough position too. Maybe not as fun as short but what the heck, the extra running might help me lose a few pounds.

Since Angie was every bit as good a player as Kathy, Kathy felt Angie was an ideal target for her sarcastic one liners, like this:

Kathy: Nice catch out there Angie. Next time, try not to make it look so hard, wouldja? I almost called a paramedic.

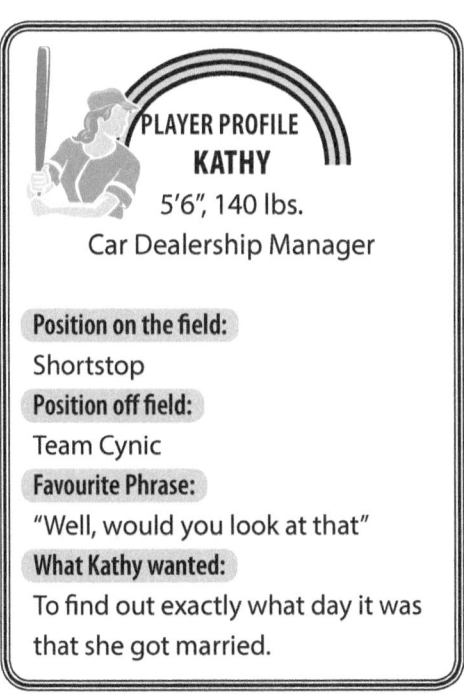

PLAYER PROFILE
KATHY
5'6", 140 lbs.
Car Dealership Manager

Position on the field:
Shortstop
Position off field:
Team Cynic
Favourite Phrase:
"Well, would you look at that"
What Kathy wanted:
To find out exactly what day it was that she got married.

Kathy's one-liners were only outdone by her base running, something we all stopped to watch. Her base running performances drew an audience because, regardless of the particulars of the play, Kathy liked to slide. She tried to claim that she slid to compensate for her slow running, but no one believed her. She really did like diving in the dirt.

Her strategy was simple. Regardless of risk, run. This approach guaranteed the necessity of a slide, or a dive into the base. Dives involved a recognizable leap off the lead foot with both arms and hands stretched straight out in front of her, and a yoga-like cobra pose midair before landing with both hands firmly gripping the base. A slide required a leg first approach similar to the cartoon illustrations of Hobbes, Calvin's toy tiger, when the two of them played imaginary baseball. Long lanky leg goes out first, the entire body airborne and parallel to the ground, one arm out and up a little like a bull rider, and then a precise fast short slide over ground as hard and sharp as a potato grater, finishing with a pop up to standing position with one foot smack on top of the base.

Whether she was called safe or out, when she returned to the bench the team would gather around her to inspect the damage. The more holes and tears in her ball pants the better to see the bloody red raspberries flashing somewhere between her ankles and her hips.

Mary:	I've got Polysporin and Band-Aids in my bag Kath. Do you want some?
Kathy:	Nah, I can't even feel it. Jesus, would you look at these pants? They're brand new for chrissakes. Hey Miller, could you get me a discount if I bought ten pairs at a time?

She would then pull out a smoke and enjoy the glory, thoroughly satisfied.

WENDY, AN ON AGAIN OFF AGAIN RAINBOW, THOUGHT BASE SLIDES and dives were foolish. When Kathy told her she would have made it to second if she had slid, Wendy said, with genuine astonishment, 'Why would I do that? I could end up with a broken leg, for God's sakes. Breaking bones isn't fun. Aren't we supposed to be having fun?' While I agreed with Wendy that the first goal of playing ball was to have fun, I, like Kathy, thought daring the opposition to beat me to a base *was* fun. I liked to win my own personal challenges and suffered agonizing frustration with my throwing, but I rarely felt upset when our team lost a game. Wendy, on the other hand, *never* allowed a loss of any kind to unsettle her nonchalance.

Wendy's pragmatic view of her role as a Rainbow and her impact on the team was admirable, as was her view of the Rainbows impact on the universe. In Wendy's world view, ball players and teams existed in order to give people something to do while the earth took care of the serious business of life, such as producing oxygen and turning on its axis. Whether Wendy hit a home run or struck out, whether we won or lost the game, whether we qualified for the Nationals or not, in the end, what difference did it really make? When we didn't make the cut at the provincials that would have allowed us to compete in the Nationals, Wendy said:

> Wendy: Well, that's too bad girls, it would have been kind of fun to go to Toronto, but oh well, we gave it our best shot.

If Kathy was in a bad mood, she might have answered:

> Kathy: Bullshit. We didn't give it our best shot, I know for a fact at least four of us showed up at the game with a hangover and I was one of them.

To which Wendy would reply:

Wendy: Well then, it's all your fault and I can forget about all my mistakes. Anyone going for a beer tonight?

There may have been one or two Rainbows who found this fait accompli attitude insufferable, but after a couple of beers they came around.

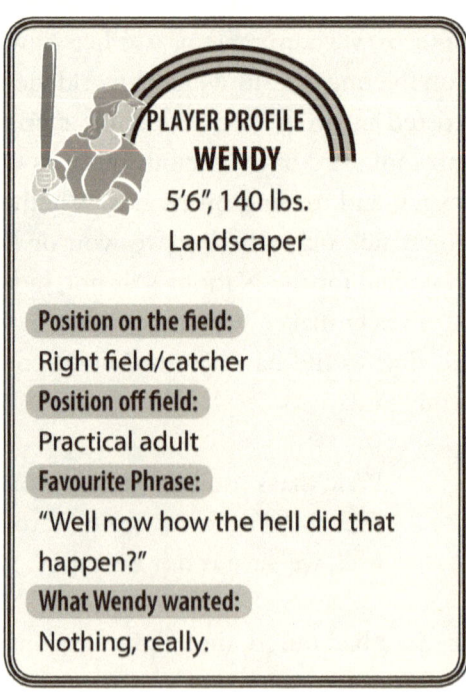

CHAPTER 15

My second season with the Rainbows followed the pattern set in the first; babysitting arrangements continued as a precisely timed scramble, and, still grappling with my throwing problem, I remained in right field.

Rainbows antics also continued to amuse and astonish me:

The summer night is warm and dry and filled with the scent of drying hay. We're in this prairie farming town for a tournament and after a great day of ball are turned out in our best jeans and shirts and standing at the door to the dance hall looking for a table. Hundreds of players and locals are two- stepping across the dance floor in the dark hot hall, but through the dim light Mary's blue eye shadow glows and Angie's pink lips shimmer. Our jeans are too hot for dancing, but at such a social event as this any other form of clothing is unthinkable. It is 1980's rural Alberta, after all. Unless you've stumbled into an actual square dance where ladies wear fluffy dresses and men wear nylon pants, jeans are *de rigeur*.

But we won't be dancing in these sweltering spa wraps, because we have no husband's in tow, and in 1980's rural Alberta, dancing with someone of the same sex is taboo. It would be another decade before our newest player Janet dragged a few Rainbows onto an empty dance floor in Waterton, Alberta, and liberated us from our own prejudices.

On this night then, the dance floor is packed with couples two-stepping to "Fishin' In the Dark", and Darlene is complaining that Will is not there to dance with her. And the hall is dark alright. As if reading my mind, the DJ activates his 70's strobe light. I have never seen straight up country folk two- step under a strobe light before, and as the light flickers and distorts my view, I wonder how they can travel around the floor without crashing into each other. Then I realize they're all going in the same direction.

Blindly I follow the team to the nearest table.

Debbie:	How about here?
Trudy:	It's too close to the cans.
Debbie:	Well, where do you want to sit then?
Kathy:	Near the bar, where else?
Sherry:	Oh come on! You guys are taking too long.

Sherry has no patience for procrastinators. As a full time single working mother, her recreation time is precious and not to be wasted. She slides ahead of the pack, Karen and Kathy quickly fall in behind and moments later their jackets hang from chairs around the end of a long table and they're standing amongst the laughing talking shouting hooting crowd lined up at the bar.

The rest of us find chairs and squeeze around the table but Angie remains standing and squirming in her Levi's to the beat of the music, clapping her hands, singing and shouting. She wants to dance.

Maybe it's a Brooks and Dunn or George Strait tune that kicks in and we trim the beer from our hips and bums and waists by wiggling and grooving in our chairs, poor substitutes for a dance partner.

Angie keeps dancing with herself, fatally oblivious to the attention she is drawing from men cruising the perimeter of the hall in their tight Wrangler jeans crumpled at their boot clad ankles and giant polished silver belt buckles lighting their way.

I see one in a Clint Black outfit spot Angie and watch him push his way through the crowd, his grin, as he draws near, revealing his chewing tobacco stained teeth. I whisper to the nearest Rainbow, 'look', and like fire the word goes around the table. Angie is snapping her fingers now, and tapping her toe, waiting for the next song to start. Sherry has shoved a beer in her hand and she takes a sip. Clint Black taps her on the shoulder and she spins around.

Clint Black:	Wanna dance?
Angie:	(Sputters) Christ no, I'm married (which is technically not true), what makes you think I wanna dance?
Kathy:	He thought you wanted to dance because you're standing there advertising yourself like a streetwalker, idiot.
Angie:	Well why can't I enjoy the shittin' music without being hit on?

She slides onto the edge of Kathy's chair but Clint Black hovers, hoping that, in this clutch of unaccompanied women, one of us will take him for a spin on the floor.

With backs turned to the desperado, Kathy lights a cigarette and he finally drifts away.

Debbie:	Who do you think will get asked to dance next?

A few are nominated, including myself.

Debbie:	Why don't we make a bet?
Karen:	I've got a better idea. Let's all pitch in a buck and whoever gets asked next takes the pot.
Kathy:	But only if you dance with the poor sucker.
Sherry:	If no one gets asked the money can go in our slush fund.

Kathy:	You mean our Slut Fund.
Wendy:	Jesus Atkins, what kind of name is that?
Debbie:	It's perfect! I love it, hahahahaha.

Next to me I hear Mary mutter, 'you guys are nuts', before taking a sip of her one and only rye and seven.

Angie:	Oh my God this is hilarious but don't tell the guys. Christ if Rob heard this he'd have a fit. Imagine it you guys, the Rainbows Slut Fund, hahahaha, it's crude but it's bloody funny isn't it?
Mary:	It's bad alright. You can count me out, Debbie.
Kerry:	Me too.
Sherry:	Hell, I'm in, come on Kerry, don't be a party pooper!
Karen:	We need some rules first. Matsumoto can't play GoGo Girl and Sherry has to stop singing into her beer bottle.
Kathy:	And you Gillingham (Karen), can't lap dance on your chair.

Slowly, loonies are dug out of pockets and wallets and a ten dollar pot appears on the table. Conversation turns to the day's game and plays are recalled, umpires are skewered, and glory dust floats seductively over our freshly coiffed hair. The DJ plays some John Cougar Mellencamp which gets me moving in my chair.

Angie:	Hahahaha, looks like Michele's after the Slut Fund!

Unprepared to dance with a stranger and imprisoned in my 1980's sensibility which won't free me to go shake my booty solo to my favourite rock and roll, I freeze.

The song ends and another two- step begins. A mature and dignified looking man approaches our table and stops behind Wendy. Hands respectfully behind his back, he bends down and asks her to dance.

Wendy: Sure, I'd love to!

She rises from her chair, adjusts the elastic waist of her sweat pants that are patterned with multi-coloured cartoon dinosaurs because she is, after all, the oldest member and therefore the dinosaur of the team, leans over the table, points at the money and warns:

Wendy: Don't anybody touch it. That's mine!

In awe we watch our practical, grey streaked short haired, librarian- like, sometime teammate being escorted to the dance floor, confident in her knowledge that her long time husband would only laugh at our inanity, and congratulate her for making ten bucks.

The gauntlet is thrown down. For years thereafter, the Rainbows Slut Fund becomes a coveted prize. New players, like Sheila, make spotting potential victims a game in itself:

Sheila: Ewwww, look at this one coming! Quite the specimen! He's heading straight for us, I think he's got his eye on you Trudy.
Trudy: I hope so, I'm broke.
Sherry: Christ, here comes a real winner. Check out the belt buckle. It's the size of a dinner plate.
Sheila: Oh my God, look at that specimen, what a hottie. Listen, if he asks one of you, I'll double your money if you let me have him.

Several seasons pass before Angie finally gets her shot at the pot.
A short, bald, lonely looking man comes up behind Angie who is sitting in a chair, and politely asks her to dance.

Angie: It's about flipping time! Christ, I was beginning to wonder if I'm past my prime.

She stands and turns, looks at the man, who doesn't notice her deflated look as he takes her arm to lead her to the dance floor.

Two songs later Angie returns and sinks into a chair across from me, her face a vision of despair. Her back straight and stiff as a bat, she stares at me while the gentleman stands pitifully behind her, his small pale hands firmly gripping the back of her chair. Guarding his prize.

Angie's big bright pink lips begin to move. Holding my eyes, she mouths:

Angie: Help. Help.

CHAPTER 16

THE SUN WAS SHINING AND THE SPRING BREEZE WAS GUSTING AND Debbie and I were warming up for a game. My frustration with the mini melon sized ball boiled over.

    Me: This ball is too big, it feels like a melon! Do we really have to use it?

Smack. The ball landed neatly in the pocket of my new glove. Over the swoosh of a wind gust I heard:

    Debbie: What?!
    Me: Do we really have to play with these ridiculous-sized balls?!
    Debbie: Yes!

I gripped the ball and positioned my wrist forward, trying to counteract the tendency for the ball to roll off the tops of my fingers when I let it go. This awkward position interfered with my arm extension and the ball went hard into the ground at Debbie's feet.

    Debbie: What the hell was that!?

Good question, what *was* that?
Concentrating, I forced my arm into a robotic performance of a throw. The ball went in a straight trajectory from my hand to Debbie. My arm retracted.
Smack.

Me: You good? I'm warm!

I wasn't warm, but if I tried another throw like that, the nuts and bolts in my elbow would have disconnected.

Debbie didn't mention the ball assault on her feet but my ego was not going to let it pass. In my ear I heard the voice of an evil leprechaun, *what was that what was that what was that!?* My intelligent, rational self replied, *it was just a bad throw. An experiment gone wrong. Forget it.* But the leprechaun wasn't having it. *Get a bloody grip on it, come on!* The miniature monster stamped up and down on my shoulder, its' absurd little feet booting me in the neck. Slam slam. Slam.

That night in bed, the nasty creature reappeared, stomping and taunting, tormenting me. Cackling and giggling as it replayed the throw over and over on my mental screen. In my tortured state I felt my left arm, hand and wrist lying like separate appendages on top of the bed cover, muscles quivering with the memory, disconnected from my shoulder and back muscles, muscles that still remembered the feeling of a good throw, a throw free of a minder, a free in the zone, throw. Those muscles quivered too, as they tried to send the memory back to the arm and hand that was clearly having an identity crisis.

For hours that cruel imp whipped me and flipped me until, exhausted, I finally fell into sleep.

Only to be awakened at dawn by a gang of magpies squawking outside my bedroom window.

Dear Ian Tyson: your song about magpies is a lie. Magpies may chirp softly under the cover of a spruce tree or wagon wheel when it's thirty below on your ranch and then in summer take off for the hills, but everywhere else, in summer, they screech and squawk like rusty metal. There is no sound in the universe so annoying, so maddening, as a gang of twenty magpies convening over a breakfast of stolen cat food in your yard at 5:00 a.m.

I flung away the sheet, leapt out of bed and flew down the hall in my baby doll pajamas. I stormed onto the deck, pounding my bare feet, smacking my hands together and shouting as I made my way down the length of the deck which ran from one end of the house to the other. From the deck railing, from the tops of lawn chairs, from spruce tree branches and the bird bath, magpies lifted off in every direction, squawking and mocking my fury. In the corner of the deck lay a triangular piece of wood cut from the 2X4's Husband had used to replace the old deck rails. In one fluid motion I bent down grabbed the wood, rose, got a magpie in my sites, wound up and let go, achieving a bullseye shot that dropped that bird straight down to the ground.

I had struck the bird dead.

I stood in horror. I had never killed a bird before. I had never killed a creature of any kind in such a violent outburst. I slapped mosquitoes, swatted flies, and squished spiders only when they were inside my house. But birds? I love birds. *But look at that shot*, I said to myself. I still had it in me! My aim was dead on! And the object was more awkward than the melon ball, it was a triangle, for crying out loud! I can do it, I can do it, I can do it!

For the next few days magpies came in silence to pay tribute to their dead compatriot, which I left in its expiry place as a reminder to the rest of the flock of the perils of using my yard for their raucous meetings, and a reminder to myself that I had it in me to throw any object of any size with deadly accuracy.

I went to my next ball game filled with confidence and hoping at least one fly came to me in right field so I could test my revived sense of athletic competence.

The bases were loaded and I was in right. All fielders had backed up to avoid a deep hit over our heads and a grand slam. The batter took her position and Darlene pitched one of her sky high lobs. The hit came fast, a deep fly to centre, sending Kerry and Debbie and Sonny all running while I headed for the space between deep centre and second base to take the cut off throw, watching all the runners on base who were waiting to make a run for it as soon as the ball hit the ground or a glove. Kerry caught the fly and sent the ball straight in to me and I turned around and saw Sherry and Trudy hanging around second base and heard them shouting…

Sherry, Trudy: Home!! Throw it home…

I wound up for the throw, everyone waiting and watching the runner trying to beat me to home base. I let go and watched in horror as Sherry dropped to the ground like lead her hands around her head. Trudy picked up the ball that would have killed Sherry if it had hit her and threw it home. I felt my body melting from the heat of my humiliation.

Sherry: Jesus Christ I said home! Not second, home!

They thought I meant to throw it to second base.
We got the third out at home and headed to the bench where Sherry and Trudy and Angie and Karen were all having a laugh. In contrast, I was trying to stop myself from throwing up.
That night in bed I seriously considered quitting. I had almost killed someone. If that ball had hit Sherry she could have dropped dead just like the magpie. This was no laughing matter. How could I keep going if I couldn't get a grip on this ball and on my psyches? I had to get over it, somehow. I had to figure out how to throw this ball. I had to get a hand transplant. Or I had to give it up and take up something safer, like darts, or water balloon toss.
To avoid any more near misses, for the rest of the year I developed a strategy. On the rare occasion that I received a ball out in right, I ran in with the ball until I could safely make a toss to Mary or Trudy. The villainous leprechaun was indignant. *You're cheating you're cheating you're cheating!*

I was able to ignore the little imp and during warm-up I began conversing with Pride, an entity that in such conditions can serve as a useful coach:

Pride: You can fix this. You must. Practice practice practice. Find a grip. You must. You must. I know you can do it. I'm sure of it. Positive. No doubt.
Me: But it's the ball! It's just too big!
Pride: Get over it! Quit the whining! Everyone else has figured it out and you can too!
Me: You don't have to yell.
Pride: It's you yelling at yourself, dummy.
Me: Right.
Pride: Come on, it's okay, you just have to relax, quit thinking about it so much. That's really the problem, you're just thinking about it too much.
Me: You're right, I really have to quit it. Just quit it Michele, quit it. I can throw the damn ball. I can I can I can.

And, slowly, throw by throw, I figured out a partial grip on the damn melon ball, so that, by season's end, I had made a few decent throws that led to successful plays that muffled my evil leprechaun. But not for long.

And miraculously, the Rainbows kept me on the team.

CHAPTER 17

When I learned that Rainbows are supposed to time their pregnancies so as not to interfere with the ball season, it was too late.

That year had not been a good one economically for our household. Canada was in a recession and it was hitting companies like ours hard. Our fledgling construction company depended on dreamers building dream homes that needed basements dug and roads built, but dream homes remain dreams when the bank won't front any of the money, and that year the banks were keeping a tight lock on their vaults.

Husband left for a few months of work in the North West Territories, and I gave in to the spectre of a red line on our bank statement and took on a part time contract with a lawyer at an all-female firm in Calgary. It was different, going a few days a week to draft Statements of Claim and Affidavits on the top floor of the low rise office building where these female barracudas were smashing the glass ceiling. I, on the other hand, was not so much as tapping on it with my baby finger.

When ball season began that year, Husband was still blasting through the permafrost up north, and I was still stickhandling my way around the shards of glass in the Calgary law office. With the end of the school year, I found a teenage babysitter to come to my house, saving me the time and trouble of delivering the boys to my parents' home in Calgary.

The babysitter was a 16 year old girl named Laura, whose mother delivered her and picked her up at our acreage on the days I needed her.

Having a reliable, exemplary, babysitter delivered to my door several days a week so that I could go to work with adults, even flesh-eating ones, was a relief too profound for mere words. Imagine the effect of this change in circumstance, just imagine how bright, how light, how blessed your world would feel if God dropped in during your Sunday roast dinner and said, "From now on, your life will be perfect. All you have to do is cook and someone else will clean up, your kids will like going to school and you won't hear a single complaint from them or their teachers, your job will give you professional satisfaction without ever causing you any stress, and you will always have time to relax and have fun. Plus, I'm throwing in an annual one month tropical vacation."

Laura was a godsend of this magnitude. She loved my kids, and they loved her. When I came home from work, the house was always tidy and clean and my sons were always content. On ball nights, not only did Laura stay on to babysit, she also made dinner *and* did the dishes. Imagine! Unknowingly, this girl made herself indispensable. She transformed my life.

And so, naturally, when Husband returned in autumn, the first thing I did was get pregnant. After all, I now had a helper! I could have as many babies as I wanted and work outside the home and the children would not become dysfunctional. Laura had saved me.

My third child was due the following July. When I informed Debbie that I would not be able to play ball next season:

Debbie:	What! Why the hell did you let that happen?
Me:	It's Darlene's fault. She said when you have the third you hit the sweet spot.
Debbie:	I thought the only sweet spot was on a bat!

When a woman is nestled in the bliss of her living and incubating offspring, winter is not perceived as something to be endured, but rather embraced. That winter, blizzards and long dark days accentuated the cozy bright bubble of joy which oozed out of me, surrounding and saturating my family in silky jelly love, creating a place of light and tenderness in our home that I filled with the scent of nourishing food, words of devotion and affection, and copious amounts of hugs and kisses. And that oozing jelly love provided, I was told, the disturbed children I continued to volunteer with a true dose of medicine so needed in their lonely hurting souls.

CHAPTER 18

THE BABY WAS DUE IN JULY BUT BY MAY I FELT AS HUGE AND unstable as one of those giant air- filled Michelin Men tethered in front of the local tire store. I felt like my child might fall out of my womb at any moment. I was so big, and heavy, and unwieldy, so bloated and swollen with water, if someone had pricked me with a fork I would have become a sprinkler for my sons to run under on those warm summer days.

At my weekly weigh in at my doctor's office the scale indicator was tilting close to the point of no return. By late June I had surpassed fifty pounds of weight gain.

Dr.'s Assistant:	Good afternoon Mrs. Veldhoen, how are you this week?
Me:	Hot and heavy thank you, and you?
Dr.'s Assistant:	Yes, you seem to be retaining a lot of fluid. Step on the scale please.
Me:	I'd rather not, thank you.
Dr.'s Assistant:	I beg your pardon?
Me:	I don't want to know how much more weight I've gained since last week. In fact, I don't think I will get on that scale again until after the baby's born.
Dr.'s Assistant:	The Doctor won't approve.
Me:	Well, since I'm now bigger than he is, he'll just have to get over it.

My antipathy to the scale extended to any 'one' or any 'thing' that I felt threatened the world peace and harmony for which I yearned. While my unborn daughter was curled up in my womb, my social conscience awoke. Love seeped into the deepest crevices of my being. I cooked and baked and decorated and hosted and said yes to every request that came my way. I had always wanted to fix the world but had never really tried. Since I could not play ball that year, I decided it was time to try.

With two toddlers and a baby soon to be born, my options were limited. I could not go to Africa and take on elephant poachers, or go to the UN and straighten out the world's dictators who hung out there, or walk across the continent to raise money for a worthy cause.

But I could write letters to the editor.

I began with a focus on local and national issues – many of which happen to be the same ones young mothers are concerned about now. I began firing off letters to the editors of various magazines and newspapers that I read while sitting in my gynecologist's office, and our rural paper that appeared in my mailbox every Wednesday, the Western Wheel. I also wrote dozens of letters to politicians and copied the editors or vice versa. I continued to write letters for more than ten years, until I put my money where my mouth was and ran for political office.

I had an opinion about everything. The proposed sex offender registry, recycling, irradiation, trans-fat, labour disputes, drugs in schools, child care subsidies, local development, the GST, the environment, family allowance, and any and all matters related to children including education, poverty, and health. I wrote to several Prime Ministers and Premiers and dozens of Ministers, my Municipal Council, the CBC, The Alberta Report, the Herald, the Eagleview Post and, my personal favourite, the Western Wheel. The letters to the Wheel were invariably read by Angie, who usually had a comment, even if the letter was published in January and she didn't see me until May.

Angie:	Hey Michele I liked that letter you sent to the Wheel about the by-law officer thing, but Rob says you guys have to do something about all the trashy properties out there in the country......
Angie:	Geez Michele I read that letter you sent about day cares. You sure do have an opinion about that, don't you?

I did have an opinion about everything then. Worse, I thought I had all the answers.

Oh, the naiveté and righteousness of young mothers oozing with jelly love.

The rest of the team rarely commented on my letters to the editor, perhaps because they didn't read the Wheel, or perhaps because they really didn't care about recycling or the dangers of irradiated food. Or, perhaps I was insulting some of them with my very definite opinions.

One letter did produce a round of Rainbows support. It was, as Angie called it, 'short and sweet':

Dear Editor:

Where is your story on Resolution One? This is an organized effort by Alberta businessmen to demand tax reform and responsible fiscal policies from our federal government. We must support it! Call Victor Olivier at 403 484 8884 and register your name! I don't know about you, but I'm <u>fed up</u> with paying for public servants turned public swindlers and <u>I refuse to pay</u> a National Sales Tax! CALL NOW!
Seriously!

I would like to take this opportunity to apologize to all those readers who were subjected to my demanding and annoying exclamation marks.

Looking at the state of the world today, it is evident that my time would have been better spent in therapy trying to fix my throwing problem. Perhaps I would have gone on to create that professional women's softball league and made billions of dollars which I could now be using to fix the world, just like Bill and Melinda Gates.

Oh well.

A couple of weeks before the birth I went to watch a Rainbows game, wearing one of the few outfits that my swelling body could fit into and tolerate in the heat - a matching top and skirt in solid watermelon red. An ensemble that should never have been manufactured as human clothing, this number did not serve to minimize the size of any of the parts on the front of my body. My normally diminutive breasts had morphed into massive and unruly blobs of flesh. My bra would have fit a nursing orangutan.

The team had just wrapped up the inning and was jogging in to the bench.

Mary:	Hi Michele, nice to see you. Looks like you're due any day now.
Kathy:	Jesus Veldhoen, get one of those fake white beards and you could be the world's fattest Santa Claus.
Karen:	Good Lord, Michele, you're as big as a whale! How ya' feeling'?

Angie had run in from left field and was passing the pitcher's mound when she shouted:

Angie:	Holy cow, Michele, where'd you get those boobs? They're bigger than mine!

Have I mentioned it was the social aspect of the Rainbows I missed most that year?

A couple of weeks later my daughter was born and later in the fall, the Rainbows threw me a baby shower.

Debbie:	Oh my god, she is absolutely gorgeous. Why didn't I get one of these, god damn it? (Debbie had two boys)
Darlene:	Why would you want a girl? Boys are so much easier. (Darlene had three boys)
Kerry:	I would have liked a girl too. I'm feeling outnumbered these days. (Kerry had two boys)
Karen:	Well Jesus Christ, if this one's a girl you can have her, I've already got one. (Karen had shocked herself, her husband, and everyone else who knew her by getting pregnant. She already had a girl and two boys).

After three hours, I wrestled back my precious bundle, thanked the team, and escaped.

At that year's annual Rainbows Windup Banquet and Roast, I received a chastity belt and a giant poster of a very pregnant orangutan under which the caption read, "WHEN YOU PLAY, YOU PAY'.

CHAPTER 19

To belong to a team is to honour the meaning and purpose of family. While our biological families are, if we're lucky, our first team, later, once we're potty trained and need a way to wear off steam, we join a sports team. The word team usually applies to sports, but, like a family, any group of people committed to a common purpose can be considered a team. Three simple but sacred conditions are necessary to create a successful team-family.

Each member must have an authentic love for the game itself, or at least an authentic appreciation for sport. The level of an individual's skill is of far less importance than this genuine love, this passion, for their game. Think of Charlie Brown. His love for the game was real, as was Peppermint Patti's and Linus', but Lucy really didn't care about the game. She joined the team only because all the other kids were playing and, being the neighbourhood bully, she needed victims. Lucy was the source of success-squashing conflict on Charlie's team.

Each member must know the meaning of commitment, and be committed, absolutely, to the team. Commitment requires the courage to defy threats of lightning, sleet, hail, spousal abandonment, whining children, ransacked kitchens, red lining budgets, rumour, gossip and innuendo. And bodily harm, of course. Charlie Brown was the epitome of commitment. While the rest of the team ran for shelter when it rained, he remained steadfast on the pitcher's mound.

And each member must be capable of seeing worth in every other member. A member may hit the ball too softly or run the bases too daintily, but if she brings to the team determination, humour, enthusiasm, style, generosity, wit, honesty, diplomacy, or creativity, she is worthy. Or organization. At least one member needs to bring organization. The organized one can be spotted at the head of the pack, leading the rambling bunch of well-dressed smart asses who are generously sprinkling the air with their wit. Had Charlie Brown been a Rainbow he might have been called a blockhead but someone would have bought him a beer after every game and given him a lift home if he needed one. And loaned him a cap that fit.

When all the conditions are met, an energy develops. An energy that flows easily from player to player, rippling across foreheads tense with worry, opening chests of optimism, hope and joy. Some would call this condition a state of grace. Life is now, life is laughter, life is a delight. The push and shove of the bigger world fades from the conscious mind.

Games will be won not because of skill alone, but because of this flow of energy. When games are lost, they are still a win because of those few carefree hours.

Such life affirming moments of harmony, hilarity, and grace came often to the Rainbows.

Travelling back in time to remember the people that have come and gone in our lives is a gratifying trip, don't you think? Rarely do we plan such trips in advance, they more often just happen with friends over a beer or cup of coffee. People we might have otherwise forgotten come tripping or shouting into the conversation and sometimes, the memory of them can truly astonish us because we can now see them with that wonderful wide open view we gain with time. I love that. When I look at the past with my older eyes.

I am taking one of those trips right now and bringing to mind some Rainbows who were short on time spent on our roster, but nevertheless, are making me laugh.

There was Peggy, a short haired, short-statured short-term player who picked off a lot of runners at first with her lightning throws from third. Her short term was not due to her short stature, but rather to a spell of short temper, which was justified because when the Rainbows were short on effort Peggy was not, leaving her feeling shortchanged.

There was Carmen, a freshly minted school teacher who mistakenly believed the founding members of the team, one of whom had been her junior high French teacher, would be great mentors and role models in sport. Being young and energetic, she kept up with us easily on the field. Being young and impressionable, off the field she thought she should try to keep up with the high octane post-game partying Rainbows, rather than the in bed before midnight teetotalling Rainbows. This effort landed her in a Vancouver karaoke bar where she gave a guest appearance with the pseudo Diana Ross and Supremes bunch and then went on to host the after-show party in her hotel room, the details of which she has paid me enough money to keep a closely guarded secret forever.

We were graced for one season with a little French Canadian doll, Micheline, whose sweetness, I thought, was in peril around the Rainbows, but, now that I know she is the President of a corporate compliance and governance consulting firm, I realize it was the rest of us who were in peril. Micheline was appreciated by incorruptible Ardith, a generous straight lace who refrained from swearing, smoking, drinking, and giving Kathy a single opportunity for a sarcastic remark, but would buy your beer all night if you asked her to.

We also had for one season an American ringer whose performance at the Quebec Nationals will always be remembered for its astounding lack of minutes actually played. Whether this was due to a seized back, or indulging in her unique choice of muscle relaxants, we will never know.

And there was long, lanky, 20 year old Shelley, whose remarkable flexibility led us naturally to call her Gumbo. But what I liked most about Shelley was her earnestness. Her sense of commitment and loyalty. Her desire to please.

Shelley:	(Straight face, low serious voice, staring you straight in the eye): Hi. How's it going? What do I need to do to help us win this game? Put me wherever you want I'll do the job.
Sheila:	(Gum in mouth). Snap snap snap. Is that chick for real?

Yes, she was for real. As were they all, unforgettably, for real.

CHAPTER 20 – Part 1

Nylon stretch ball pants are forgiving pieces of clothing. Long before spandex and Lululemon, female ball players had figured out the advantages of stretch pants. Aside from their durability and resistance to ripping during a slide, these pants allow for monthly bloating, changes in shape of aging bodies, and excessive consumption of nachos and beer.

All of which I cared about not a whit. I wanted ankle length cotton pants, like the ones the professionals wore. I thought our knee length, thick nylon stretch kelly green ball pants were hideous.

Feeling secure in my membership on the team, I began an annual appeal to change this aspect of our uniform. I was humoured, but never taken seriously, which proved to be a good thing after I gave birth to my third child. The fifty plus pounds I had gained during the pregnancy went away, but left my body in a different shape that only those dreadful nylon ball pants would accept.

And so, when I got out on the field in the summer of 1989, I looked like a new woman.

I also felt like one.

Darlene had been right about hitting the sweet spot with baby number three. With my daughter's arrival I felt my parenting skills shift smoothly into drive, and my maternal engine was performing at its peak. Adding to my sense of achievement was the easy integration of my oldest son into kindergarten at a school that was proving to be a winning example of a team. A family.

My cup was overflowing.

This feeling of abundance, competence, and control, miraculously transferred onto the ball field where I found myself easily throwing the melon ball. Plays to first, to second, into home were on target, my grip on the ball firm. I had broken the barrier, I was back to my old self! I felt as light and nimble as a fairy, gliding and leaping, swooping up balls and sending them floating to the infield straight and sure as a lazer.

The team saw the new me too, and so I was put in centre field to fend off our strongest league rivals, the Mavericks, who had hatched a plan to take the league championship that year, a title to which the Rainbows had become quite accustomed.

Their strategy was simple. Stack the team with plenty of heavy hitters who could send the ball deep into the field, giving their runners time to get around the bases. This offensive game plan required the Rainbows to reconsider our defence. Since I was fast on my feet, I was moved over to centre field where I worked that fairy magic. I had been put in cold and didn't choke. Hallelujah. Even the evil leprechaun was speechless most of the time. Occasionally he found his voice but I would grit my teeth and make the throw and with my inner voice shout at the little brute to get lost. (It's true, even my inner voice never used the F word).

Our defence had been working well and, although the Mavericks had won a game or two, we were still ahead in the league rankings when I almost killed Red.

Our bench was short that game and since I had been giving such stellar performances in centre I was put in left field.

Left field. Left. Not only is left *the* field, but it is also directly behind short. As I jogged across the infield toward my position in *left*, and crossed the baseline between second and third, I felt high octane fuel lighting my torch of secret dreams. *Ah, short, my love, I'm coming, I'm coming.*

Like a cat sneaking up on a gopher hole, I sniffed around my hallowed field until I found the precise square foot of grass on which to position myself. I punched the pocket of my glove, yanked up the knees of my hideous nylon pants, leaned forward, and prepared to meet my destiny.

The first few innings went well. The Rainbows kept up a solid defence, picking off the fly balls and line drives, and scoring some runs with a strong offence. However, the opposition had managed to hit a few out of the park, keeping the score close.

Now, we were at a crucial moment. A heavy hitter was up to bat, there was a runner on third, and we could not afford to let her get home.

Crack! The ball was coming straight to me, and I watched its beautiful trajectory up up up as I adjusted my position, calm and confident. This was one of those balls that fielders love and batters hate to hit – I barely had to move, it was as if the batter intended to hit the ball right to me.

Smack! Into my glove and I started running in fast, telegraphing to the runner on third, *I dare you I just dare you I dare you to try to make it home I'll have the ball to home plate before you can say Bob's your uncle.*

Red, the runner, looked over her shoulder to check my position. On the nearby bench her teammates were shouting, "Run! Run! "Go!" and the evil leprechaun hanging onto my ear lobe was whispering *hahhaha now you're in it look at everyone watching waiting for you to mess up.*

Red ran. Took off at a full lope (that's horse talk for gallop but I like lope better), I wound up to make the play, my eyes lazer focused on Sheila's glove which she had somehow managed to position over the plate while extending her arm and body at least twenty feet away, like she had a telescopic arm. I could see her jaw motoring up and down at top speed working her gum to work off her fear. I let go of the ball and drilled it straight down the base line. And into the back of Red's head.

Crack!

Oh my God I've just killed Red!

So why is she still running?

Red crossed the plate and turned toward her bench, laughing and poking her hands into her massive nest of red hair, which spread and fell around her shoulders and down her back. The 4x4 sized wooden hair clamp that kept it bundled had been smashed by my ball.

My life, and Red's, were saved by ten pounds of hair bundled together with a two pound wooden "accessory." Back in the field my body trembled like a leaf in the wind. My throwing arm felt like a lead weight. Perhaps I could have it surgically removed and replaced with a new one. One that came with a programmable feature with options that included warnings such as, 'Abort the throw, abort the throw!' The evil leprechaun leapt on my moment of weakness, occupying my entire skull, straddling his legs over my pony tail, arching his back over the crown of my head, draping his arms around my ear lobes, and picking his nasty pointy little teeth right in front of my eyes.

Sigh.

One bad throw and I was tossed back into that slimy, algae choked slough of despair.

PART 2

A WEEK HAD PASSED SINCE THE NEARLY KILLED RED INCIDENT. A week in which every night in bed was movie night and the only film showing was Nearly Killed Red. My leprechaun was in charge of the projector and he had it on automatic rewind. On the other side of our king-sized bed Husband snored obliviously, while my leprechaun ground his puny little heels into my self-image and dipped his dirty smelly toes into my shrinking pool of confidence.

A conversation with one of the 19th century's famous psycho-therapists such as Sigmund Freud may have rescued me from the pain and agony of my throwing problem. Freud might have suggested I had a fixation:

Freud:	You seem to be fixated on the *size* of the ball.
Me:	Well it's too big, especially for my hand.
Freud:	What size of ball would you consider appropriate for your hand?
Me:	The one that's used in fastball.
Freud:	As I'm not familiar with the game, could you compare the size of a fastball to something? Perhaps a clementine, or a man's testicle?

Perhaps I had buried some sort of traumatic memory that was corrupting my ability to throw. There were nights when

I excavated deep into my mind looking to root out any such memory, but when I got too close to that box in which we all hide our secrets, I bolted out of the pit. I knew what was in that box. I didn't want to let it out.

Other nights before closing my eyes I lectured myself about the uselessness of searching. *Not tonight. NO reruns. You are taking this thing waaaayyy too seriously. You have got yourself in a knot over one bad throw. Think of all the good plays you have made. Think of all the catches, the hits, the runs home, and get over it for God's sake!*

Determined to fall asleep to sweet sounds and thoughts, I would close my eyes and imagine a spring breeze whispering in the poplars in my yard. When the breeze turned to a cold north wind I would imagine my children's heart- melting smiles. When the smiles turned to crying and wailing, I resorted to counting sheep, knowing perfectly well I would soon be leaving the bed and reading on the living room couch until I could no longer keep my eyes open.

Exhausted and defeated, I dragged myself to the next game.

I sat on the bench under a cloud-streaked light blue sky waiting for Debbie to finish hanging the bat bag on the backstop. Behind me trucks rumbled into the parking lot, cleats clicked on the pavement as players ran to their diamond, and all around me Rainbows chattered and cracked spits.

Me:	Debbie, can I talk to you a minute?
Debbie:	Oh Christ, you're not going to tell me you're pregnant again are you?
Me:	Haha. Not a chance. I'd like to try a different position. How about I catch?
Debbie:	What?! Why would I put you there? We need you in the field.
Me:	Well you can play field too. You've been putting yourself on the bench a lot, I should sit out more.

Debbie:	What's the matter? Don't you want to play?
Me:	I just need a change.
Debbie:	If it's your throw last week forget it. It happens.
Me:	I thought I had a grip on things.
Debbie:	You do. Quit thinking about it so much.
Me:	Easier said than done. I'd like to sit out or just catch for now anyway.
Debbie:	I guess we can mix things up a little. Let me think about it.

A few minutes later, Debbie called out the line-up and positions:

Debbie:	Mary, first, Kerry, rover, Sherry, pitcher, Sonny, left, Michele, second....'

Second! I glanced at Trudy, whose hold on this position, I thought, was permanent. She was tipping her travel mug up for a drink and appeared unruffled.

Second. I can handle second. Sure I can. Yes, I can. I jogged onto the infield for our pre-game warmup, assessed the distance between first and second base and chose a point midway and behind the baseline to position myself. Nerves tingling, stomach gremlins bouncing, I hunched over with legs apart and rested my ball glove on my knee, trying to look ready.

Crack! Debbie started her rounds of the infield with a hard grounder to Karen on third. The ball tore straight up the baseline and took off past her and out to Angie. Another hit and the left side of the infield was in the groove, firing off their throws to Mary at first.

My turn.

Crack! The ball smacked the ground and came straight at me. I bent down eyes on the ball, glove out and ready, but the ball bounced high, and like a hammer, pounded into my jaw.

I staggered to the bench the team running in behind me.

With a blue plastic cold pack pressing against my throbbing jaw, I watched the practice from the bench, waiting for my pain and humiliation to subside. Since when couldn't I pick up a grounder that took a bad bounce? What had happened to my reflexes, my hand eye co-ordination?

Determined to ignore the obvious, I joined the team at the Lazy L after the game, but when I could not open my mouth to take a sip of beer, I capitulated, turned down all offers for an escort to the hospital, and took myself to a clinic, where I discovered I had a fractured jaw.

Doctor: If you promise me you'll stay off the ball field for the next 6 weeks, I won't wire your jaw shut. You should be able to chew soft foods in about a week. But if you get the slightest bump on your jaw, the hairline fracture will turn into something much worse and then you will be wired up and living on liquid food for 6 weeks. Your choice.

By the time I got back on the field 6 weeks later I had resigned myself to the fact that I was no longer the player I once was. Or thought I was. Never before had I critically assessed my athletic skills. Now, my leprechaun and I were furiously conducting an assessment in my head. While I was telling my children every day, "You can do it, you can do it!, you can do whatever you want to do if you try hard enough!" I was telling myself, *you can't throw you can't throw you can't throw.* My leprechaun vigorously nodded in agreement.

At times my determination felt like a form of self-punishment. *Why are you doing this to yourself? Why don't you give up ball and take up something easier, like knitting?* Then I remembered how hard both my grandmother and Brown Owl had tried to teach me this simple craft, and how, despite hours of effort, I was unable to achieve my knitting badge. I really wanted that badge because all the other Brownies had theirs. That poor poor, Brown Owl. Her efforts to teach me were deserving of a medal. I actually had private knitting lessons with her, something I doubt any other Brownie anywhere could claim. She did eventually give up, inspiring my first true cynical thought. *If she can't teach a left hander how to knit what good is she?*

I turned from knitting to my old dream of playing tennis. When I was a teenager I had always wanted to play tennis but kids my age then were preoccupied with other pursuits such as toking up.

I arranged a tennis game with the only person I knew who had an interest in tennis, my friend Vera. Vera agreed to play with a beginner because she hadn't played in years due to a chronic case of tennis elbow. We met at the old cracked court in Okotoks; she brought the balls and me a racquet. After a few minutes of basic training, we got started. I managed to get the ball over the net and so she suggested we move back to the baseline and rally from there. This worked well until Vera's tennis elbow kicked in. 'Damn it', she muttered, rubbing her arm. 'Well Michele, I'm done. It looks like I'm stuck with this elbow thing again. Sorry about that, sweetheart". Vera called everyone sweetheart.

Perhaps there was a name for my problem too? Softball Arm? Throwing Disease? Adult Onset Hyperkinesis?

Looking back, I would now call it Psychogenic Hypochondria.

At the Rainbows wind up that year, my award was a face mask. Custom designed with green ribbons and streamers and my number 25 plastered on either side.

CHAPTER 21

Most women (and possibly some men) reading this will be familiar with the Cotton Pony Club. For those who are not, the Cotton Pony Club is the club women join once a month, like it or not. When women are 'riding the cotton pony' they are menstruating. Yes, the term is crude, unladylike. Coarse. Something a rapper might come up with. Yet back in the '70's, long before rap, Carol Burnett used the term, along with the associated "inner bitch", and if one of the Queens of Comedy was using those terms in the '70s, there are likely new ones in use today that you and I don't know.

For me though, raised by a mother who never discussed the topic, the term 'cotton pony', and the way the Rainbows used it, was a revelation.

The Rainbows were in Sylvan Lake, Alberta for a tournament. Weather conditions were ideal for inner bitches expecting the appearance of their cotton pony. Cold and wet.

We had arrived early on Saturday, driving through a steady light rain to make our first game scheduled for that morning. In Sylvan Lake the rain was heavier and looked socked in, but the tournament organizers asked all the teams to give the weather until noon before making a decision to cancel or proceed with the games.

Karen had brought her camping trailer earlier in the week and set it up near the ball park. We were all in her trailer, cold and damp, drinking coffee, and waiting.

Sherry:	Christ, I hate Sylvan Lake. Whose idea was this anyway? This place has always been a bug infested swamp.
Debbie:	Oh shut-up Sherry, it's not. And how is anyone supposed to know in February what the weather's going to do in June?
Sherry:	Like I said, the place is a swamp regardless. It was stupid to sign up for this tournament.
Karen:	Jesus Sherry, you must be riding the cotton pony. Here, take a pill, will ya?

I had no idea what the cotton pony was and at that moment was afraid to ask.

Sherry:	I'm not riding the F**** cotton pony! Yet!
Kerry:	(Under her breath) Yikes.
Sonny:	How about some Kahlua in your coffee, Sher?

Trudy stepped out of the washroom:

Trudy:	God damn it, my period's started. Does anyone have any tampons?
Mary:	Oh boy, here we go.

Mary pulled her emergency pack out of her sports bag.

Angie:	Jesus, I better check my calendar, maybe I'm due too.

She flipped through her little black book.

Angie:	Oh good, I'm not due 'til Monday.
Karen:	How the hell can you be so precise?

Angie:	I don't know, but it comes like clockwork, always has.
Debbie:	Mine too, more or less.
Trudy:	There's only two in here Mary. Does anyone else have more?

I spoke up:

Me:	I've actually got mine right now too so I should be able to give you a couple.
Sherry:	Well why didn't you say something sooner for Chrissakes!
Sonny:	Here Sher, have some more Kahlua.

Now clued in to the meaning of cotton pony, I began to understand why the team tolerated the occasional cattiness from each other. They were allowing their inner bitches an opportunity to expel all the hormonal vinegar that builds up throughout the month.

The morning wore on with no let up from the rain. Debbie draped herself in a slicker and went out to find out what was going on with the tournament.

Sherry:	If they don't cancel this thing, I'm outta here anyway. This is ridiculous.
Trudy:	I'm coming with you. No way is the diamond going to be any good any time soon, even if the rain stopped right now.
Angie:	Oh come on you guys, don't be such party poopers. If the rain stops by noon we'll be able to play this afternoon.
Karen:	You just wanna stick around so you can strut around in left field and pick up some more bragging rights.

Mary:	Whoa, let's be nice now girls.
Kerry:	I think there's too many hormones in here.
Karen:	Jesus Christ, you're right Kerry. It's that time for me too, but I thought the bitchiness was finished. Guess not.
Angie:	Maybe we should compare calendars before we book tournaments. Hanging around with all your bitches is no fun.

The trailer door opened and Debbie dripped in.

Debbie:	Jesus Christ, listen to this. The diamond's under a foot of water but they say they're going to wait another hour and if the rain doesn't stop, we're going to have to play anyway. They said they won't refund our money if we don't play. Can you believe it? Plus, my god damn period just started!

Sherry, who was still wearing her brand new pair of white Levi's, leaped up from her seat.

Sherry:	Well that's just bullshit. I'm outta here girls.
Debbie:	Sherry!! Your pants!

Ah, the blessings of womanhood. Sherry hadn't jumped atop her cotton pony quick enough.

Angie:	This is shittin' amazing! Maybe I should get ready just in case I join the club early which would be the first time in my life it came early but you never know this might be contagious.

An hour later we were huddling under a tarp draped over our dugout trying to watch through torrential rain as Kerry stood in a pool of water and took the first swing at a pitch she couldn't really see.

The Rainbows Cotton Pony Club continued to experience extraordinarily well coordinated meetings throughout the duration of the club's career. Based on our record, it would seem women with synchronized cotton pony arrivals are destined to make a good ball team.

CHAPTER 22

LIFE NEVER STAYS SWEET AND EASY FOR LONG. HOW CAN IT, WITH the infinite ways in which we can suffer? Jobs are lost, loved ones die, divorces happen, hearts are broken. There are arguments, refusals, rejections, betrayals, and old unresolved hurts haunt us.

But all of that is a walk in the park compared to sick children.

On a frigid winter night, Josh, now four years old, wakes me from a deep sleep. In the shadows he stands calmly next to my bed.

Me: Josh, what's the matter?

Josh shakes his head.
I sit up on my elbow, peer at his face.

Me: What is it honey?
Josh: I can't breathe.

I strain to hear him, he sounds like a strangled Darth Vader.

I surge up switch on the bedside lamp and look at him. His lips are blue and his face is white.

Five minutes later our truck disappeared in a haze of vapour and swirling snow as Husband and a wrapped up and strapped in Josh, headed for the city. Terrified, I dialed 911 to alert the emergency department of the nearest hospital which is half an hour away.

Due to his astronaut quality composure and sheer stoicism, Josh was able to keep a sliver of airway open long enough to get to the hospital where he was immediately encapsulated in a giant tent filled with lifesaving oxygen. A fact I did not know until Husband called a couple of hours later.

Husband:	Hi.
Me:	What's happening?!
Husband:	Nothing much. He's sleeping inside a big oxygen tent. He's fine.
Me:	What happened?
Husband:	The doctor said he had an asthma attack.
Me:	An asthma attack? Why?
Husband:	I don't know.
Me:	You mean you didn't ask?
Husband:	No, I didn't. The people here were kind of busy saving his life.

An asthma attack. He could have died, the doctor later informed us. For the second time, Josh had flirted with death. The first time, at age two, was not an acute event but rather a slow decline in weight and health until he was finally hospitalized to be poked and prodded by a variety of specialists all of whom were stumped and seriously worried. After almost a month in hospital eating nothing but rice Pablum, banana, and grape juice, he developed a bacterial infection and so was given a simple antibiotic which miraculously and unexpectedly cured him.

I had thought at the time, *Well, I've had my crisis with this one, he should be good now until he's on his own.*

Oh, the naiveté of a young mother.

The next evening, Josh was home happily playing with his toys as if the previous night's brush with death had never occurred. In contrast, the trauma was still playing out in my body as I shakily fiddled with inhalers and capsules of steroids the contents of which must be mixed into his food, the thought of administering to my little boy such potent drugs causing my instincts to flail in protest.

A few weeks later, when Debbie hosted the Rainbows next season planning session, I was still trying to figure out how to mend the cracks in the shield I believed I had built around my children.

The last to arrive, I slipped into the sunken living room and settled onto the fireplace hearth. The whole team was there along with one or two faces I didn't recognize, and the house was noisy, everyone talking, laughing. I sat quietly with my brooding mind.

The team was catching up on news, and the conversation turned to kids.

Kerry: How are your boys, Michele? How does Ben like kindergarten?

The subject of my first child in school switched on my inner pride light. Ben was a kindergarten star, a kindergarten superhero, a kindergarten genius. He could assemble *all* the blocks into a cohesive whole, he could write his *whole* name, tie his shoes, knew his pleases and thank yous, he was the cutest, brightest, best.

Oh, the seduction, the shame of such pride, such ego. I tried not to give myself away, but my enthusiasm knew no limits. With a brand new baby and a four year old, I had become a Milk Mom and volunteered for the Home and School Association, becoming a member of the Board. Unwittingly, I had jumped with both feet into the role of SuperMom.

Me: Oh, he loves it. His teacher is wonderful.
Debbie: How's Josh? Is he jealous of the baby?
Me: Sometimes, but nothing serious.

I took a deep breath.

Me: Josh was diagnosed with asthma a couple of weeks ago. He woke up in the middle of

	the night and couldn't breathe. Scared the hell out of me. Now I have to give him all these drugs which I hate doing.
Debbie:	Oh shit. I know that feeling. Marty gets croup. Scares the shit out of me too.
Karen:	Did I hear you say Josh has asthma Michele? Stephen did too when he was little.
Angie:	Yeah asthma isn't any fun. I hear it feels like choking.
Kerry:	So what happened Michele? Is Josh okay now?

Kerry, the great listener, knew. I unloaded my fear and worry, I let in the medicine.

There was so much more to being a part of the Rainbows than playing ball and enjoying an after game beer.

ON A COLD CALM EVENING LATER THAT WINTER, WHEN I HAD adjusted to having a child with asthma, I was in my kitchen storing ten pounds of leftover beef stew in the fridge and listening to a CBC radio program when I discovered a potentially permanent solution to my Psychogenic Hypochondria.

I joined the family in the living room where my three for the moment contented children were on the floor pushing toy bulldozers, building Lego castles, and, in the case of the littlest one, crawling over Husband.

Me:	Hey, guys, do you see pictures in your mind?

My sons, adorable in their matching train and truck flannel pajamas, were engrossed in castle construction.

Me:	Guys?
Guys:	Huh?
Me:	You know, if you are telling me about, say, when you rode your bike through a big puddle, do you see a picture in your mind of you on your bike?

Blank stares and silence.

Me:	Okay, work with me for a minute here. Everyone think of an apple. A red apple. Thinking of a red apple? Okay, now, can you see the red apple in your mind? Do you have a picture of it in your mind right now?
Husband:	No.
Me:	You're kidding! Really? You actually cannot see an apple in your head right now?
Husband:	Nope.
Me:	I can't believe it! What about you Josh, do you see the apple in your mind?
Josh:	No.
Me:	Are you sure? Close your eyes, try to see a shiny red apple.
Ben:	I can see it.
Me:	Oh thank goodness, I was beginning to think I was crazy. Can you turn the apple around in your mind Ben?
Ben:	Uh huh.
Me:	Can you cut it with a knife? Right now, I'm cutting mine with a knife and the juice is spritzing my hand.
Ben:	I'm cutting mine too.
Josh:	Is Ben allowed to use a knife now Mommy?

Discovering the concept of visualization *as a deliberate action* was a revelation. The hot topic on the news at the time, I listened in amazement to radio hosts interviewing guests talking about visualization as a tool to reach your goals. With focus and commitment to regular sessions of visualization, anything can be achieved, the experts claimed. Want to win a 1500 metre foot race? Picture yourself, arms and legs pumping, eyes straight ahead, passing your competitors, and crossing the finish line. Do this enough times and it will happen for real. Want to learn how to speak Mandarin? Imagine yourself conversing fluently with a bunch of Chinese businessmen gathered around a bar knocking back cocktails and signing deals. Want to lose twenty pounds? See yourself in a size six designer gown floating around the dance floor at your company Christmas party. The experts claimed that regularly creating and referring to such visuals in your mind will help you reach your goals.

I had been seeing pictures in my mind my entire life. Multiple times per day, the inside of my head spontaneously combusted into images. When listening to a story, my mind created a movie to match the words. I even saw actual words in my head. Whole sentences! Wasn't this normal? Didn't the inside of everyone's head become a movie theatre when someone was telling a story? Sometimes the show was so good I could pull up a lounger and settle in with a bucket of popcorn. And when I was thinking ahead, planning the weekend, or a special event, I pictured every detail. Didn't every home cook see in advance what her Christmas feast would look like all laid out on a long tablecloth clad table, shimmering bowls of homemade cranberry sauce, steaming scones, scented pine boughs and all? Couldn't everyone see flickering candlelight and a steaming cup of tea on the ledge of their bathtub, and bath bubbles squished up around their neck? These visualizations occurred spontaneously in my mind. It had never occurred to me that I had any control over them. I visualized difficult moments too. Conversations I needed to have with my exasperating grandmother, or Husband. *Husband, could you please leave your muddy boots in the garage? Please? How am I to teach the boys to help keep the floor clean if you don't leave your muddy boots outside?* Rehearsals of such dialogue took place in my mind and included body language and facial expressions. When I tired of those rehearsals, pictures of me at the grocery store, or the post office, would appear in my mind. Those films were B grade and boring but I had to lie down and concentrate on stopping them. Finding out that other people had to concentrate on creating images was a genuine surprise to me.

I began to understand that visualization had been my way of preparing for much of my everyday life. This was a revelation.

Although my mind movies occurred spontaneously and were for me natural and, I thought, uncontrollable, I tested my ability to imagine pre-selected images. Snow falling. Yep. Star hopping. Yep. Rolling dough. Yep. Rolling joints. Yep. Why did I picture that? I had never rolled a joint in my life. Right, I could picture whatever I wanted, whether I had experienced it or not. I recalled that, as a young child, I loved to go to the top of the street upon which we lived, imagine myself a bird taking flight from the light post there and, as I ran back down to our house, fly home.

I absolutely believed I was flying.

And of course, later on in my childhood, during every softball season, I envisioned myself as a grown-up, professional ball player. A shortstop. On the field in white cotton ball pants.

Excited at the possibilities of using visualization to control my mind and overcome my throwing problem, I advanced immediately from cutting apples to throwing the melon ball. In my mind I created and played a faultless video of myself in my hideous nylon kelly green pants, acing throws from field to first base, to second base, to third base, to home. I followed the advice of the visualization experts and set aside time just for this self-affirming mental exercise, settling into a nightly routine of lying flat on my back in bed with my arms straight at my sides. Despite the fact that my left arm and hand responded to my virtual throws by literally stiffening into a useless inoperable angle, it never occurred to me to seek help to unlock it. Unfortunately, none of the Rainbows suggested I seek out a sports psychologist. I suppose even if they had wanted to send me for professional help, it wasn't in the team budget, and the slut fund was winner take all.

But my eternally optimistic nature had me convinced I had discovered the cure for my Psychogenic Hypochondria. Visualization, I told myself, was my ticket out of right field.

Despite the Nearly Killing Red and Sherry episodes, I told myself, the past season had gone well and with visualization, I would vanquish memories of those terrifying moments.

I began my new Visualization Program the year we went to Quebec for our first Slo-Pitch National Championships.

CHAPTER 23

CROOKED STREAKS OF NEON BLUE LIGHTNING WERE STABBING THE sky. We were at the bottom of the inning and up to bat. The season had started off well. Although we had lost a game or two to the Kinfolk, their strategy had backfired. Instead of buckling, we had stepped up our game and were playing better than ever.

Angie:	That lightning's getting closer.
Trudy:	Yeah, too darn close for me.
Sonny:	Ah, come on, don't be such wimps. A little lightning never hurt anyone.
Karen:	Oh really? Weren't you hit by a bolt of lightning just before you got married?

I turned my back against a blast of wind just as Debbie, who was up to bat, took a swing at the watermelon the pitcher had just tossed her, then turned back to watch the ball sail straight over second and into centre field.

Crrrraaaack!

Karen:	Lordy, you chumps can pretend that was the sound of Debbie's hit, but I'm gettin' out of here. Lots of room in my truck.

As players raced for shelter, fat blobs of rain began splatting on the ground, setting off puffs of red shale dust. Thunder growled inside the black cloud now positioned over the field.

Debbie: Someone grab the bats!

We wrapped up the nylon bat bag, hauled it to the back of Debbie's truck and chucked it in before piling into her suburban.

Debbie: Listen to that rain!

Kerry pointed southeast.

Kerry: Looks like hail over there.
Debbie: Shit, Brian'll be having a fit.
Mary: What's he got over there, Debbie?
Debbie: Canola. Thank God for crop insurance.
Kerry: Amen.
Angie: Hey Debbie, can I help out at your branding this year? I'm dying to go to a branding, I've never been to one but I hear they're a blast. I know I'll have to help cook and everything, and you know me, I'll be in there like a dirty shirt…
Debbie: You'll have to eat prairie oysters.
Angie: Really! Do I have to?
Debbie: Anyway, you'll have to ask Brian.
Me: What are prairie oysters?
Kathy: Don't tell her Miller, just invite her to the branding and give her some.
Debbie: Never mind about brandings. Listen, there's a tournament next month that we need to go to. It's a qualifier for a new national program set up by the National Slo-Pitch Association. Anyone wanna go to Quebec?
Mary: Quebec?? To play ball? Why would we go all the way to Quebec to play ball?

Debbie:	Because it would be fun! But first we have to qualify. Which means we have to go to this qualifying tournament next month and do well enough there to go to Provincials. Then we have to place at the Provincials to qualify for the Nationals. And then we would have to book tickets for Quebec next summer, doesn't that sound like a hoot?
Angie:	Oh yeah! Why not Mary!! That would be so much fun. We could drink French beer, do they drink beer in Quebec? I hope so, I don't like wine besides it doesn't go very good with wings, but I wonder if they even eat wings, they're kind of food snobs aren't' they? What's it called? Hot coozeen or something. Anyway I'm in!
Debbie:	Jesus Angie. *Haute cuisine.* What about the rest of you?
Kathy:	I'm in.
Trudy:	Sounds good to me.
Kerry:	How long would we be gone? I'm not sure Jack could handle eating at Chung's every night for more than a week. I'd have to find a sitter too.
Debbie:	Let's take the guys with us. They can be our bat and water boys. And we can share a sitter.
Kathy:	Have you checked with Sherry and Darlene yet? We can't go without a pitcher.
Debbie:	I asked Sherry, she's thinking about it. But she'll come. We'll need Darlene too. It's on the agenda for our post game meeting at Lester's.
Trudy:	What about you Michele?

I heard the echo of my name in the time tunnel I had been travelling through since hearing the words 'Nationals' 'and 'Quebec'. For months I had been diligently visualizing myself as a star ball player and at that moment I was back in Christina Lake, catching and throwing balls from short to first and on the bench the coach was popping the lid off her ice cream bucket full of orange slices. I was pedaling my sparkly purple banana seat bicycle down the road from the ball diamond at top speed so I could let go of the handlebars and coast through another warm summer night filled with infields of hope and outfields of dreams.

Me: I'd love to go, but I'm not sure it'll be possible.

The conversation I would have to have with Husband had already started to appear as dialogue in one of my mind movies. The dialogue ended with: "I don't know what next summer is going to look like yet. I'll have to wait and see."

The storm passed, ball players were appearing back on the diamond, Rainbows were climbing out of Debbie's truck.

Back out in centre field the dialogue kept popping into my mind.

Me: The team wants to go to a national tournament in Quebec next year. But we have to qualify first.
Husband: Oh yeah.
Me: If we make it, most of the Husbands are going to come.
Husband: Oh yeah.
Me: So, what do you think?

Several options presented themselves at this point in the dialogue:

Option 1:	Not much.
Option 2:	I can't go to Quebec in the middle of summer.
Option 3:	How long will the trip be?
Me:	Probably a couple of weeks at the most.
Option 1:	Hahahha.
Option 2:	Why so long?
Me:	Well there's no point going all the way to Quebec and not taking some extra time for a vacation.
Option 1:	I don't have time for vacations in the middle of the summer.
Option 2:	I don't know what next summer is going to look like yet. I'll have to wait and see.

A Kinfolk batter stepped up to the plate. There was a runner on first, we could get a double play. Sherry tossed a spinning fat pitch, the batter went for it. Crack! The ball ripped off the bat and sailed toward the now clear and jeweled blue sky in left field. Sonny started a backward side stepping run while I ran hard to cover her, something I had to do while knowing she would never miss the ball. Kerry and Debbie moved in toward second to cover Trudy for the throw that would be coming once Sonny caught the fly. The ball was coming now and the runner had taken off from first and was heading for second, she was getting closer and Kerry and Debbie and now me, were all converging around the base. The runner went down for a slide, Trudy reached out to catch Sonny's throw, then bent and turned to tag the runner she knew was there.

Like a train wreck the line of Rainbows toppled over the sliding runner, Trudy being the last car to flip sideways and go down. Under the crumpled pile of bodies the Kinfolk runner managed to hook a finger onto the second base bag.

Umpire:	Safe!
Sherry:	Bullshit!
Sheila:	Holy crap. I'm glad it's not me under that pile of flesh. The only thing that would have survived is my hair.

This may suggest we were not fit for a national competition, but we didn't think so.

Later at the Lazy L Debbie filled in the rest of the team about the Slo-Pitch National program.

Karen:	Quebec! Christ, will they let us in? We don't speak French.
Kathy:	If they know what's good for them they won't let us in even we do speak French.

WHEN I GOT HOME THAT EVENING, I FOUND HUSBAND DOING SOME earth moving with our bobcat. Mia, now two years old, was in her car seat strapped onto the side of the machine. Josh was gleefully hosing down a wasp nest and Ben was atop the John Deere lawn tractor, studiously cutting the grass.

Although on ball nights I was still making my timed-to-the-second runs to pick up the neighbour babysitter, occasionally Husband was able to take on child care. On those evenings he taught Ben, and later Josh, how to drive our John Deere ride on lawn tractor. With the boys now aged seven and almost six, Husband felt both were old enough to start doing useful things, like mowing the grass.

I looked at the scene that evening and said to myself, imagine. If I wasn't playing ball, these kids would all be freshly bathed and tucked into bed. And missing these valuable life lessons. Every seven-year-old child, after all, deserves an opportunity to learn how to drive a John Deere lawn tractor! Learning this crucial skill now means that by age 10 he will be able to market himself as a professional, and by age 16 he will be able to support himself which every 16 year old should be able to do, right?

When I confronted Husband with this sarcasm, and expressed my fear that Ben may tip the tractor over and be crushed under the machine, he insisted this was not possible.

Me:	What if he drives in the ditch the wrong way and tips?
Husband:	Michele, the ditch is as flat as a pancake. How could he tip?
Me:	He's only seven! Anything could happen!
Husband:	Nothing's going to happen except the grass is going to get cut while he's having the time of his life.

I stood and watched my son. Under his man-sized John Deere farmer's cap his little boy face was the picture of concentration, what you might see on the face of a nuclear physicist handling uranium. As the neon orange sun descended in the sky behind him, he steered the tractor in a ruler-straight line toward me, following the cut line from his last pass. His speed was about two miles an hour.

He drove right up to me, turned off the engine, lifted his foot off the brake pedal that Husband had modified to accommodate a child driver, and, with a grin the size of the moon said to Husband:

Ben:	Can I do the other side now?
Husband:	Not tonight Ben, it's time to shut 'er down.
Ben:	Can I do it tomorrow?
Josh:	No! It's my turn! When can I do it?

Me:	You're not old enough yet! You have to be at least six before you're allowed to drive! (this would actually be the case in September). It's time for bed guys. Leave your shoes and socks and pants in the garage and get ready for the bath.

As I started unbuckling Mia, I said to Husband:

Me:	The team wants to go to a tournament in Quebec next year. They're thinking the guys should all come and we could make a bit of a vacation out of it.
Husband:	Hehehehe….
Me:	It may not happen, we have to qualify at the Provincials and we have to qualify just to get to the Provincials. Anyway, I'd love to go.

Business had taken off since Mia was born. Acreages were popping up like mole hills and we were digging basements as fast as meerkats dig holes. (I like to imagine both domestic and foreign forms of wildlife for my similes).

Me:	You should come. You'd have a blast with the other guys and you'll need a break. It's been so busy.
Husband:	Next year's a long ways away.

Well, that was a start, I thought.

CHAPTER 24

THE SKY OVER THE BALL FIELD WAS GREY AND THREATENING RAIN. Medicine Hat sits on flat treeless prairie and enjoys hot summers long enough to grow big fat delicious ears of corn. Ball tournaments there usually happened during a heat wave when the only water around was the sweat on our bodies and the drinking supply in our team water jug. This weekend had been hot too but humid, classic pre-storm summer weather on the prairies.

Earlier in the season we had executed Debbie's plan and qualified for the first ever, Slo-Pitch National Canada's Provincial Championship Tournament, being held in Medicine Hat. The competition was fierce, but we had been playing at the top of our game and were now in the final, vying for the gold medal, and therefore already qualified for the Nationals in Quebec.

I was back in right field for the tournament and had been getting as much action as all the other fielders. The teams we had been playing all knew how to place their hits and the women we were up against now were pros, putting their hits deep, then shallow, then up the baseline, then up the middle. Out in right I was doing a dance before every hit, deciding on the best place to position myself.

On the bench Ruth had been tracking each batter's hit, looking for patterns.

Ruth: Back up Michele, this one went deep last time!

Debbie: No! The bases are empty, stay in and cover Mary!

I picked a spot in the grass, already slick with humidity, and with the hem of my shirt wiped the sweat from my face.

Spit.

Spit.

Spit spit.

The batter went left, her hit down and dirty up the third base line, eluding Karen and skidding out on the grass toward Sonny, who picked it up and fired it into second, holding the batter at first.

We were at the bottom of the last inning and up just one run. Our opponents were on their last bats. If they scored one run we would have to battle through an overtime inning to get our hands on the Championship, but if they scored more than one run we would lose, taking home the silver medal. Naturally, we were aiming for Gold.

I looked up at the sky.

Spit spit.

The light sprinkling of rain was just enough to make the grass slippery. A fact I only discovered when I started running for the ball that had just been hit between right and centre where Debbie was running. We were both heading for the ball, but I was faster so was expected to get there first.

My feet went out from under me, I landed on my side, slid across the grass. I watched Debbie retrieve the grounder and make the throw to second, and reminded myself to visualize this eventuality with a better outcome.

As I jogged back to my position in right I visualized a trip to Sport Chek Monday morning. I was selecting a new pair of cleats.

Craack!

Another grounder, hard up the middle this time between Sonny and Kerry and Kerry was ripping toward it. She's got it in her hand but the runner was fast, and already at second.

The rain now a steady drizzle.

The situation was critical. None out and two runners on base. The infield held them to first and second but one good hit and they could both be home.

A lefty was up to bat. This one hadn't shown any inclination to go anywhere but to my field. Her last hit went high and deep. The odds were good she's coming my way.

Debbie: Back up Michele!
Mary: Be ready Michele!

Craaack!

The ball was rocketing straight up but light years from the deep field. I began running for the ball, I saw Mary equivocating. Should she move out toward the ball or count on me to make it back in time? As I hit my top speed she moved back to her base. The ball was entering the atmosphere again, I was almost there, the ball, dropping into range, smack! It was in my glove. I began running toward the baseline with my sights on second to make the standard play, but Trudy wasn't at her base waiting for the ball. The infield, like a frozen stage scene, how to make sense of the tableau....

Debbie: Send it to Mary, send it to Mary!
Mary: Here Michele here!

Wow! I didn't know Mary could yell that loud. Her voice broke the impasse in my brain, I threw her the ball, she caught it, put out the runner at first who had left the bag before I completed the catch. Ha! She thought I wouldn't catch it, she had to go back and tag up, the runner on second had to go back to tag up too, but now she was closing in on third. Mary threw the ball to Karen. The ball in Karen's glove, her glove on the ground, the runner was sliding in...

Out!

The Rainbows had just completed a triple play, ending the game and winning the title of Provincial Champions!

The field erupted with shouts, all of us running and in Angie's case leaping toward the bench

Angie:	WE WON! WE WON! WE WON! WE WON! WE WON!
Kathy:	Jesus Christ Angie, stop yelling, we know we won.
Kerry:	What an awesome triple! Nice catch Michele.
Debbie:	Thank God you listened to Mary.
Mary:	Good job Michele.
Trudy:	Holy shit what a game girls! Congratulations everyone, wow we were good!
Angie:	We were better than good, we were hot, we were smoking hot, we were shittin' hot, we were hotter than a hot stuff thingy ….
Kerry:	Oh boy, here we go….
Karen:	Okay, okay you bunch of farts. Can we get out of this rain now?

As I write this moment of Rainbows history I am filled with nostalgia. My skin and bones are flushed with memory, I can feel the smile on my face lengthening the lines around my eyes. A sense of grace that visited the Rainbows in abundance that night in a 16 seater Budget Rent-a-Van while we barreled home along the TransCanada Highway. That night, had you been floating over the southern Alberta prairie in a hot air balloon, you may have been forced off course by powerful sound waves emitting from that van full of damp drunk women communing with Lionel Ritchie. Dancing On the Ceiling. Feet on ceiling. Oh What A Feeling. Our glee was hemispheric.

Philosophers—Rumi— they say never look back. Do not dwell in the past, for to do so is to chain yourself, imprison yourself in a nonexistent place, thereby making nothing of the only time there is, the present. But is it not the memory of better times that helps us through the bad ones? When we need to, can we not draw close to those memories and laugh?

I keep these memories nearby, so I can include them in my daily thanks for not only this day I woke up to but all the days of my life. And sometimes, like now, I dwell there for a bit of extra bliss.

And if Rogerio is anywhere near I'll grab him and tell him some outrageous Rainbows tale, or about one of my favourite characters. Like Sheila.

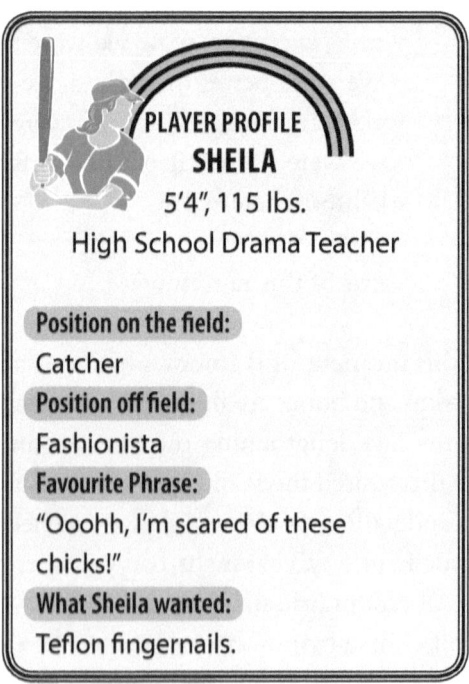

PLAYER PROFILE
SHEILA
5'4", 115 lbs.
High School Drama Teacher

Position on the field:
Catcher
Position off field:
Fashionista
Favourite Phrase:
"Ooohh, I'm scared of these chicks!"
What Sheila wanted:
Teflon fingernails.

Sheila had a completely unrealistic expectation about ball. She felt her nails and hair should stay in-tact while playing. She was vigilant in her efforts to maintain them during a game but despite this, she was a brilliant addition to our team. Her t-shirts and her teeth were both a brilliant white, and she was usually laughing at something, including her own jokes. Around Sheila, I could only stand in awe of her honest observations of life. While I practiced political correctness, she practiced comedy.

When Sheila saw a ladies slo-pitch team of Amazonian sized players, she stopped chewing her gum.

> Sheila: Holy shit, no way are those specimens real women!

Sheila had a petite and delicate body which did not reflect her personality. Discovered by Debbie in the early 90's, she played with the Rainbows until she left Okotoks about five years later. Her profound impact on the Rainbows in those few years can still be seen today, particularly in the areas of fashion conscious athletics, and sports commentary.

Since Sheila was a drama teacher, her sense of style was evident even when she wore a ball uniform. Carefully selected nail colour, makeup, hair style, and jewelry nicely complemented our green and white look. Her commentary during games went something like this:

> Sheila: Holy moly, these ladies are so big I don't need sunscreen.
> I shouldn't have had so many fried onions on that burger. The poor umpire's afraid to lean over me cuz he knows he might get gassed.
> Holy crap, take a look at the one wearing shorts. Her leg hair's so long I could barely see the plate when she was up to bat.

Her comedic contributions to the Rainbows legend came naturally to her. Playing ball did not. Why would Debbie invite someone to join the team who considered a morning of fingernail filing more important than a ball practice? But Debbie knew what she was doing. A recreational ball team could have enough athletic talent, but it could never have enough renegades and comedians. Sheila was both. She was young, single, and brimming with enough energy and imagination to take on Eddie Murphy and Robin Williams at the same time. Like a ground squirrel in summer, she popped up and down on the field, taking a look at life and squealing with delight before disappearing again to check on the kids who received the briefest of visits before taking off across the field in chase of a cute boy squirrel.

At weekend tournaments out of town, Sheila saw the Saturday night party as an opportunity to exhaust herself of all her vitality. Which is to say she had her share of drinks. We all know that comedians and artists often hit their creative peaks with the influence of some kind of drug, and Sheila was no exception.

At the Sunday morning games that followed such nights, Mary would take stock of the team before setting up the lineup.

Mary:	How are you feeling today Sheila?
Sheila:	I felt fine until I woke up this morning and realized I was still alive.
Mary:	Oh yeah? What's the matter?
Sheila:	I'll let you know as soon as I figure out how to remove my head from the rest of my body.
Mary:	Too many drinks last night?
Sheila:	Not enough. I should have had one more to finish myself off and save myself from this misery.
Mary:	So I guess that means I should put someone else in to catch this game?

Sheila:	Well, you can put me in if you want but the ump will have to throw the balls because if I move too much I'll puke.

On better days Sheila entertained us with her attempts to hit the ball and get on base. Standing in the batter's box vigorously snapping her gum and looking perfectly turned out in the uniform which she wore with the poise of a Chanel model, she chopped delicately at the ball, usually managing to make contact by the third pitch. She would then begin her run down the baseline to first, in the style I always imagined Tiny Tim when he sang "Tiptoe Through the Tulips". Sheila's hit would often peter out somewhere in no man's land between third, short, and pitcher, a result which, if not for her being desperately in need of swing improvement, could be mistaken for a strategy. The defense was never sure whose ball it was to play, resulting in a surprising number of safe-on-firsts for Sheila. Once installed on a base, she blew a bubble and checked her nails. If any were damaged she could be heard cursing. Next, she checked her helmet hair for correct position, and about then we would all hear Mary yell, "Run Sheila!" to which Sheila responded instantly, with the intent of making it to the next base without breaking another nail.

CHAPTER 25

I WAS IN MY KITCHEN ON A HOT JULY AFTERNOON, SNIPPING THE ends off a bushel of green beans. This is a mind-numbing activity. The beans were from my garden where they were multiplying faster than Pokémon's, due to the ten foot deep layer of decayed cow poop in which they were planted. I had been up to my ears in green beans for a week and was filling a corner of one of my 25 cubic foot freezers with them for winter consumption. This was when I was still fiercely committed to Real Turkey. Real Vegetables, home grown without chemicals, were equally important.

I heard a knock on the door at the bottom of the stairs that led up to the kitchen from the walk out basement. Then I heard the door open and Debbie yelling. "Michele? You home?"

I came to the top of the stairs and looked down.

I was surprised. Although I had grown accustomed to country people dropping in on neighbours unannounced, Debbie's home was too far from mine for her to be considered a neighbour, even in the country, and she had never before come to my house other than to pick me up and drop me off once for a tournament.

Me: Come on up, I'm just blanching beans here.
Debbie: What? Blanching beans? You're kidding!

She came up the stairs in her slow steady style and followed me to the stove where I was about to lift another batch of bright green beans from the boiling water. She looked at the sink brimming with beans cooling in ice water.

Debbie:	What the hell are you doing with all these beans?
Me:	I'm freezing them.
Debbie:	You're nuts! You know you can buy them frozen in the store?

We laughed, I offered her a cup of coffee, but she said she couldn't stay.

Debbie:	I was just coming back from town and remembered I promised Brian I'd bring him and Marty lunch. They've been haying a field down at Policeman's Flats since six this morning. Shit, they must be starving by now. Do you have some sandwich meat and bread?
Me:	Sure. How many sandwiches do you need?
Debbie:	They usually eat three each.

I pulled a package of deli ham from the fridge and a loaf of bread from the freezer.

Debbie:	Do you have any white? Brian doesn't like brown bread.
Me:	Sorry, I don't.
Debbie:	Oh well, he'll get over it.

As we stood side by side smearing the bread with butter and mayo and mustard, I felt the kinship that comes after enjoying good times and a couple of crises with a team. And I knew I was no longer just a Rainbow for a few months each year. By being called upon to supply this lunch, I was being christened a true member of the rural community of which the Rainbows were such an integral part. I was helping to feed a real live farmer.

Murray McLaughlin would be proud, I thought to myself. I was doing more than just waving at the dusty old farmers I passed on the road. I was actually making one of them lunch! Maybe the grain that went to the flour mill that went into the bread I was lathering with butter came from his farm! Yes, it could be and that would mean the circle was complete, and I was right smack in the middle of it!

Debbie:	Is Mia napping?
Me:	Yeah, she went down just before you got here.
Debbie:	Damn.

We packed the sandwiches into a big plastic bag.

Me:	Here, take some apples too.
Debbie:	They won't eat apples. Do you have any cookies?

Prairie farmers, apparently, don't really like fresh food for lunch. Just give 'em a slab of well-preserved deli meat slapped between a couple of slices of plain bread, lather it up with all the condiments in your fridge, and throw in some good old fashioned Dad's Oatmeal Cookies and they're happy.

I stood at the kitchen window and watched Debbie stroll to her pickup, her hips rolling the way a relaxed and confident woman's hips should. She popped the big bag of sandwiches and cookies into the back, climbed into the driver's seat, and drove her quarter ton truck at a respectable speed down my gravel driveway. For a moment I watched the ensuing dust hang in the hot summer air. For another moment I wondered at the way things were. Debbie was a teacher, she had the summer off, but still she had a job to do, feeding her farmer husband and their two sons. She did this work faithfully and with ease, but never allowed this duty to interfere with her chosen summer recreation, the Rainbows.

I too, had an air of independence about me. I had chosen to be a full time mother in an era when most of my peers were pursuing professional careers or travelling the world. I was blanching green beans while they were bleaching their hair under a Mediterranean sun. I was keeping an eye on my two boys playing outside and waiting for my daughter to wake from her nap while they were sleeping off a night of Greek ouzo in an Athens hostel.

I heard Mia singing to herself in her crib. Liquid love flushed through my veins. I went to welcome her back into a beautiful summer day. Into our own little circle.

CHAPTER 26

Me:	So, it's time to book flights to Quebec. Are you coming?
Husband:	Who else is going?
Me:	Everyone, I think.
Husband:	Is Brian going?
Me:	Yep.
Husband:	When is it again?
Me:	August.
Husband:	August.
Me:	Yes. August.

This was not the dialogue I had visualized. I booked two tickets before Husband could change his mind.

I grew up watching my father travel the world from his recliner. He read National Geographic and kept a world map on the wall of our family room. That map drew me like lamplight draws a moth. Like the moth flitting in and out of the centre of light, my imagination flitted in and out of Moroccan bazaars, Egyptian ruins, and secret passages inside English castles. The yearning I felt for these places excited me and filled me with anticipation, because I believed then that all I had to do was grow up and the path to exotic places would open before me.

By 1991 I had yet to wander through a castle or bazaar, but Quebec at least offered architecture older than Fort Calgary.

It also offered French Cuisine.

I had started exploring world cuisines in my own kitchen, spending hours concocting the dishes of other cultures. By the time my children were old enough to order their own burger and fries, I had introduced them to vissychoise, moussaka, and an Italian layered vegetable casserole with which I tried again to convince them of the worthiness of eggplant. I had also offered each of them their own whole, completely whole, fresh (steamed) lobster, which actually had a terrorizing effect on Mia. I realize now that such a presentation on the dinner plate of a three-year-old was perhaps not the best way to introduce a child to seafood.

By the time the Rainbows Quebec tour was booked, my palate was prepared to experience the ultimate Montreal Smoked Meat sandwich, which my research told me was served at Bens. I visualized myself sitting in Bens, Montreal's most famous purveyor of the popular meat, a six inch high pile of shaved smoked meat stuffed between slices of freshly baked light rye bread topped with a slice of kosher dill pickle the size of a buffalo tongue.

I was also anticipating chances to discuss with Quebecers the ongoing political debate about Quebec's role in Canada. Although Quebec was still four years from their 1995 referendum on whether or not the province should separate from Canada, I had been following the bombast of the various separatist party leaders since the 1980 referendum, and had a strong opinion of my own on the issue. Which could basically be summed up with one rhetorical question: Are you nuts? With this viewpoint, I anticipated earnest discussions with locals from whom I was ready to learn the real story of Quebec.

SEVERAL TEAM MEETINGS WERE HELD THROUGHOUT THE WINTER to plan this first national tour. By spring, we had booked our tickets and were thinking about entering the Okotoks parade for no other reason than to toot our own horn.

Heading out to our last meeting before league play began, I went into the living room to say goodnight to Ben, Josh, and Mia. Freshly bathed and playing quietly until bedtime, they kept on tinkering with their toy machines and unicorns as I kneeled down on the floor.

Josh: Where are you going Mommy?
Me: I'm going to my friend's house. Where are you going Josh?

He pushed his toy tractor across the carpet and over my lap. At age six he had acquired real life experience driving a lawn tractor.

Josh: I'm going to the shop to check the oil!

He kept pushing his toy across the floor, coughing. The combination of pollen in the spring air and a mild cold had activated his asthma. Before bed, he would take another dose of medicine from his inhaler, along with another steroid in capsule form that my family doctor has insisted he take. "Over my dead body", I had said to the doctor. "If you don't give him this it will be over HIS dead body", he had answered.

I admired my son's strong and wiry little body and marveled at his sense of survival. As a toddler he had survived a long illness and tests for diseases such as cystic fibrosis and beaver fever, which involved being hung upside down like a leg of lamb or being poked with various sized needles. Then, at age four, the asthma attack that turned him into a blue Darth Vader. I was fairly sure this child would survive to adulthood.

Me: Josh, come here and give me a hug!

He steered his toy tractor around a wide swath of carpet, parked it in front of me, threw his arms around my neck, squeezed hard and dropped back to his knees. I picked up Mia, who also had not been well lately. I tucked her in myself before leaving.

Down the country roads I ripped, my big old boat of a car floating in the sea of gravel, dust flying behind me, a smoke signal, winter was over, our season opener was a week away and in August we were going to Quebec! All winter I had visualized myself giving star performances on the field. My confidence was high.

I turned onto the highway leading to Okotoks and stepped on the gas, cranked up the radio and let Tom Cochrane blast over the sound of the wind whipping around my ears.

Me: LIFE IS A HIGHWAY, I WANNA RIDE IT ALL NIGHT LONG…

Only a Canadian could have written that song. Tom, thanks for that one, it's gotta be the best cruising down the highway song ever conceived.

The meeting was underway when I arrived, the girls snacking on bread bowls of mayonnaise with some spinach mixed in and catching up on news.

Debbie: Come on in, nice to see ya!
Karen: Hey Michele, how ya' been?
Kathy: Yeah, how the hell are you, haven't seen or heard a thing from you for months.
Angie: Yeah Michele, how come we never see you all winter? What do you do anyway, besides write letters to the editor? I read that last one about the nuisance by-law, I kind of agreed with you but Rob didn't. He says some of those places out in the country look like dumps but Rob can be pretty darn fussy about yards and stuff. You should see the way he gets his shorts in a knot if the

	neighbour doesn't cut his grass every two days like he does. Anyway, you look like you haven't gained a pound all winter! How old are you turning this year anyway? You should be getting fatter like me, god damn it.
Kathy:	Yeah Matsumoto, you're looking a little chubby around the middle there, maybe you should try one of those shrink wraps.
Angie:	Haha. Thanks a lot Kath. I've been trying to get back in shape but between me and Rob's going-ons we're out every night of the week curling or playing hockey or volunteering with the Lions and every time I say okay just one beer after … and you know what happens. Hey! Did I tell you we joined the Lions Club? Christ, those old-timers have some social life. No wonder they're all so potbellied! Speaking of which, look at this girls!

She slid out of her chair and went down on the floor on her hands and knees.

Angie:	Look at my gut! I have cougar belly! Rob said a couple of months ago it was even swinging back and forth just like a mother cougar.
Kathy:	Holy shit would you look at that.
Mary:	Looks like you're gonna have to give up beer for a while, Ang.
Angie:	I know! I'm going on a diet starting first thing next week! I just have to get through this weekend, I'm going to two brandings plus there's a fundraiser I'm helping out at.

Sherry:	When are we getting on with this meeting Debbie? I'm tired, I can't hang around here all night looking at cougar bellies.
Debbie:	Okay, so you guys, you know our bench was a little short last year. We've only got 11 players right now. We need to line up a couple more at least, especially for Quebec. I've got one girl in mind, she's new in town. But I'm not sure you guys will approve.
Sherry:	What's the matter with her?
Debbie:	She's never played ball before.
Mary:	Never?
Debbie:	No. She's not exactly an athlete. She's actually a drama teacher.
Kathy:	Oh good, just what we need, another drama queen. Hey Angie! Looks like you're gonna have some competition!
Debbie:	She's just such a hoot. She said she would be okay with being second string, or whatever, she just wants to get to know some people and have some fun.
Trudy:	Hell, why not? I'd rather have someone with a sense of humour who wants to learn. You've got my vote.
Debbie:	Okay, I'll let her know then. Her name's Sheila. She said she would come to Quebec with us as backup. Diane and Roy and Angie H also said they'd come, so we'll have quite the entourage.
Trudy:	By the way girls, for those of you who may not know, Larry and I split.
Karen:	No shit!
Kerry:	Yikes. Are you okay Trudy?

Trudy:		Yeah, I'm pretty good actually. We get along better than ever now. We have dinner together with the kids every week. They seem to be okay with it.
Kathy:		Nice. Marriage without the strings.
Karen:		What about your old man, Atkins? Seen much of him lately?
Kathy:		Yeah, just the other night, as a matter of fact. (Takes a long drag on her cigarette). He looks the same as the last time I saw him.

My mind shifted from the team banter to the contemplation of marriage. Marriage has been compared to a dance, to the planets, to war. It's been called a prison, a refuge, a necessity, a social construct designed by men to oppress women. It's been called the highest human spiritual pursuit. By 1991, the year the Rainbows embarked on their first national tour, I had been married 9 years, but had not come to any philosophical conclusions about it yet. I was working on one though.

I kept working on a philosophy for the next 15 years, but only recently have I come to think of marriage as a ball game. In a ball game, sometimes you make the play, sometimes you don't. Some of those plays are spectacularly successful, leading to double and triple plays while others fail equally spectacularly. Sometimes you hit a homer, sometimes you strike out, and sometimes you are benched for an inning, a game, or even an entire season.

Sometimes you quit. Sometimes you come back, sometimes you don't.

Just like in a ball game, the most you can do in a marriage is give it your best and accept the outcome as gracefully as possible.

Trudy had said she and her husband got along much better as friends than as husband and wife. I wanted to ask her what had led to their marriage in the first place. I had wanted to ask her that.

CHAPTER 27 – Part 1

IN 1991, THE AVERAGE WESTERNER COMMENTING ON *LA BELLE province* would likely hit on any of three topics: a) maple syrup – *the only good thing to come out of Quebec* b) separatism— *the sooner the better* c) transfer payments—*I'm sick of working half the year to support those ###!*

These sentiments were usually expressed by a husband after gulping down a beer and always followed by a round of satisfied guffaws after which the conversation would move on to topics of real importance: hockey or trucks for the men, and family or a little town gossip for the women.

Few of the people I knew, including myself, had ever made a trip to the province of Quebec. To most Albertans, Quebec was a foreign country full of people who, during the 70's oil boom, came in droves to Alberta looking for work in the oil patch and settled in cities like Calgary, but, since they were unable to speak English and most Calgarians were unable to speak French, little cultural exchange occurred. There were a few highbrow steak houses in Calgary which tried adopting a distinctively 'fine cuisine' atmosphere, but those snobby waiters with pony tails and white napkins draped over their arms were quickly put in their place when they called a cowboy booted oil baron "Monsieur", and stated, with nose in air, that they would be happy to procure a necktie for the Monsieur before seating him.

The oil barons I knew in those days did not care for neckties.

By 1982, the oil rigs were on the auction block and western Canada was in recession. Understandably, the Quebecers went home. Not too many years later, the CBC was covering the rise of Quebec's newest Separatist Party, the Bloc Quebecois. Westerners were split into two camps. Those in favour of French Immersion in school, and those ready to engage in civil disobedience if one more Alberta dollar was included in the equalization payments scheme that sent all Alberta's money to those traitors in Quebec. ★ (Disclaimer: This sentence was written to convey the sentiments of the times, and does not represent the opinion of the author.)

By the time the Rainbows arrived at Montreal's Duval airport, the Bloc Quebecois cauldron of potions and spells concocted to brainwash the population into another referendum on separation, was bubbling nicely. The political power hungry oppressors responsible for this witchcraft were stoking the fire with softwood lumber, perhaps from Alberta or BC, and were being featured in the national news often enough to penetrate the minds of even the most staunchly nonpolitical, party hardy ball players. ★ (Claimer: This paragraph was written to convey the opinion of the author).

Due to the perceived sensitivity of Quebecers and encouragement from our French teacher guide, Debbie, most Rainbows had attempted to learn the fundamentals of polite French discourse, such as the simple please and thank you that will usually suffice as social lubrication when one is seeking food or shelter.

And so, we were keen to practice our *si vous plait* and *merci,* but first, we had to get the team in our two rental vans out of the airport traffic circle.

Ensconced in the back of the lead rental van I searched out the window for signs of French culture while Husband, the designated navigator, instructed Debbie's husband, the designated driver, to go around the traffic circle one more time while he figured out which exit to take. It was midday, and we expected to arrive in old Quebec City in time for a night of revelry after which we would spend a couple of days sightseeing before heading to the tournament town of Grand-Mere, which has since apparently been absorbed into Shawinigan.

Debbie:	I don't think the guys know where they're going.
Me:	Husband's really good with a map, he'll figure it out.
Sherry:	Can he read French? Did you notice all the signs are only in French?
Debbie:	No they're not!
Angie:	Sherry's right! Look at all the hyphens and little fancy thingy's over the letters, I'm no letter to the editor writer but I know what English looks like and that's not English, that's for sure!
Debbie:	Oh for chrissakes you guys, we're in Quebec, what did you expect? Those are French town names.
Angie:	Aren't' we supposed to be bisexual, I mean bilegal, no what is that word….
Kathy:	Hahahaha, I've been wondering about you all these years Ang, now I know…
Karen:	I'm having second thoughts about this trip, Debra. And it's not because I don't speak French. It's because I don't speak Angie.
Angie:	Very funny you guys, you know what I mean. So what's going on anyway? I feel like we're going around in circles, Jesus, I'm thirsty, I was hoping to have a beer before my next birthday…
Sheila:	We are going around in circles, actually.
Debbie:	Do you guys want some help up there?
Husband:	No no, we've got it handled.

Debbie:	I think we've gone around this traffic circle four times.
Karen:	Nope. Five times.
Debbie:	Oh for chrissake, give me the map you guys!
Husband:	Hang on, I think I've got it now.
Karen:	Six.
Debbie:	Brian!
Brian:	Okay okay.

Finally emerging from the traffic circle onto the right road, we bounced along the highway and, just after sunset, stormed the fort of old Quebec City. Traffic slowed to a crawl. We opened our windows and let in the warm night air and sounds of throngs of tourists quaffing drinks on sidewalk patios, strolling cobblestoned streets, stopping to examine statuesque street performers posed on corners as still life characters from Mars or ancient Rome. Between centuries old buildings now housing pubs and restaurants narrow alleys were lit with spotlights under which beret topped artists dabbed paint on canvasses and street stalls sold souvenirs. Music and high voices floated in the air and through all this life and celebration wafted the scent of fried bread and sugar. Old Quebec City did not smell like French fries or tourtiere. It smelled like beavertails. How much more Canadian can you get?

We had chosen as our accommodation the historic Clarendon Hotel, located in the heart of the old city, below the mount of Chateau Frontenac. We felt this was a natural choice for a ball team comprised of refined individuals such as ourselves.

The clerk at the desk, however, did not feel the same. His professional attire reflected the elegance of the lobby, glittering gold cufflinks below glittering crystal chandeliers. He scanned our blue jeans, t-shirts, and running shoes. His face fell.

Us:	Bonsoir, we have a reservation under the name Miller. We're the party of 25.
Clerk:	Bonsoir, are you sure you are in the correct establishment?
Us:	Yes, this is the Clarendon?
Clerk:	Oui, madames, but perhaps you are mistaken as to the name of your destination? If you would allow me, I will investigate and quickly arrange for more suitable accommodations for your party.
Us:	Look, here is our confirmation, take a look at your records, you should have ten rooms set aside for us.

The clerk glanced down where he no doubt saw the big block of rooms that he had been waiting to fill all day.

Sheila approached the desk, eyes flashing. She wanted to brush her brilliant white teeth, put her peculiar spaceship like lift in her hair, and get out into the throng.

Clerk:	Perhaps you would care for a refreshment in the lounge while I review our room availability?
Sheila:	What! Are you saying our rooms aren't available?
Us:	We're working on it.
Clerk:	Oui oui, may I suggest a refreshment in the lounge while I prepare the documents?
Sheila:	Non non, why don't you just give us our keys now and prepare the documents while we get prepared in our rooms?

Wendy had now joined the inquiry.

Wendy:	Hey, what's the hold up, I'm getting hungry!

Behind us, the Rainbows and Husbands were beginning to gather, sticking noses, and glasses, and bright pink lips over our shoulders. The clerk's face paled.

Clerk:	Oui, yes, certainly, you must be very hungry after your long journey.

Suddenly, he had in has hand a collection of key card envelopes, and was placing a registration form on the counter.

Clerk:	Madame, if you would be so kind as to provide me with the details of your vehicles outside, and your name and credit card, I will proceed to distribute the room keys. Your companions may come at their leisure this evening to complete their registrations.
Sheila:	Good move buster, here, let me help you…

Sheila reached forward and coaxed the key cards from the clerk and proceeded to hand them out. The madding crowd melted away and the clerk at the desk, well, he may have had to take a nip of cognac to recover his composure. Clearly, Sheila was going to be an asset to the Rainbows.

Thirty minutes later we were at a pub testing out our freshly minted French.

Rainbow #1:	BonnjOOR!
Rainbow #2:	Bonnjer!
Rainbow #3:	Bonnjoooer.
Debbie:	It's night time you guys! Say bonsoir!
Rainbow #1:	Bonnswa!

Rainbow #2:	Bonnshwa!
Debbie:	Oh for God's sakes, forget it. You're hopeless.
Karen:	Well, pouley poo poo to you too Miller!

Scattering across old Quebec City from the Place Royal to the Chateau Frontenac, the Rainbows jigged and tripped into the warm summer night, snagging such treasures as self-portraits in caricature and key rings with miniature maple syrup bottles. A few like me disappeared onto flag stoned paths and passages, through squares anchored by cathedrals and chapels, and with increasing awe and disbelief that this place was in Canada, arrived on the Rue Champlain below la Citadelle, where my recent study of Canadian History came alive.

I gazed at the St. Lawrence River below me and imagined British warships tacking against the breeze, aiming their cannons up at the massive stone fort above me, behind which the French defenders waited. This battle here, 250 years earlier, between the French and British more or less clanged the final bell, ending the rounds that had been going on between the two in their struggle over which of their nations would dominate this part of the New World. Since then, the French and English haven't stopped fighting, but only moved the battle ground into Parliament, where they employ different weapons, such as threats and dirty tricks. Sometimes they meet at nice hotels near pretty lakes and play nice, but rarely do both sides come away satisfied. The taunt of butchering each other's language has not helped either case. None of this conflict requires the Canadian population to sign up but sign up we do, since every nation appears to need something to fight about. While one might feel this aspect of nationhood to be unfortunate, I say families that fight can at least make up, but strangers that fight go for the jugular.

A shout from somewhere in the dark above me broke into my imaginings and I turned and looked up. Within a tiny square backlit opening high in the gigantic dark stone wall of la Citadelle waved an arm. I waved back and shouted.

Me:	Hello!
Soldier:	Bonsoir! How is your evening then?
Me:	Great, great!
Soldier:	Soon I will be like you, walking out in this fine night, wait for me, wait for me!
Me:	Hahaha! Okay, okay!

The soldier shouted something in French, something that felt like Enjoy! Life! Love!

Further up the Rue Champlain I stepped from the stone walk onto a broad grassy knoll where pairs of lovers were stretched out on patches of grass, perhaps with a bottle of wine tucked between them. I was on the Plains of Abraham where Wolfe and Montcalm came to blows. I considered the current love-making on this same hill and imagined a couple, one English, one French.

Him:	Let's go to Maman's for dinner Sunday?
Her:	As long as she doesn't serve pork pie again. I'm really done with pork pie, Bernard.
Him:	But it is so good, so good!
Her:	Not. Why don't we invite her to our place and I'll do up a nice roast and some yorkshire pudding.
Him:	Maman feels your roasts are overdone and yorkshire pudding, well, there is little point in making it. She won't eat it.
Her:	Hmmpf. Well, her pork pie pastry is too thick and she puts waaay too much spice in the filling.
Him:	Oh, mon cher, let us not talk this talk anymore, hmmmm?

Her:	Fine, but I'm not going to your mother's for another pork pie dinner.
Him:	Non non, no more pork pie, now come closer, come here, I have something much tastier for you my love.

Ah, if only such willingness to get along had been in the air that night in 1763…

Back with my team mates amongst the bars and pubs and street performers and crowds I had my opportunity for a serious conversation with a real live Quebecer. At a sidewalk table with the sounds of Bruce Springsteen wailing "Born In the USA", we waited for a server.

Waiter:	Bonsoir, how are you this evening?
Me:	Great, merci. And you?
Waiter:	Fine, fine, what can I get you?

We all ordered beer and when the waiter returned I put to him the question burning in my mind.

Me:	So, what do you think about Quebec separating?
Waiter:	It is our destiny, it is just a matter of time.
Me:	Why?
Waiter:	Because it is the only way to protect our language, our culture.
Me:	Why is that? It's survived quite well for hundreds of years, what's different now?
Waiter:	There are so many new people coming here, every day, we must establish, we must insist Quebec remain French.

Me:	But if people want to be French, they can be French, regardless of anyone else around them, can't they?
Waiter:	I must take care of my customers, excuse me.

Halfway through my beer he was back, squatting down next to me.

Waiter:	Yes, of course, we can and will always be French in our hearts, but we will become a minority in our own home if we don't become a sovereign nation.
Me:	So then how come you're playing all this American rock instead of Celine Dion?

I admit this was an extremely ridiculous question but by then the beer had taken hold and I was enjoying the night in that particular way one begins to enjoy such a night after drinking half a pint of beer, and therefore, I could not think of something more intelligent to continue my side of the argument.

The waiter scoffed at me.

Waiter:	This is a ridiculous question.
Me:	Yes, you're right, but really, if you can be next door to the U.S.A and be surrounded by American pop culture and still be French then what is the problem with English Canada? I just don't get it.
Waiter:	Mmmmm, well, excuse me again....I will be back to explain....

But we wandered off before he returned, floating in and out of pubs and alleys, leaving the question of culture to be answered by dazzling acrobats and gourmet French toast which I devoured sometime after 2 a.m. at a wrought iron table in a medieval looking lane.

Tired and satiated, we zigzagged a path back to the Clarendon, passing Rainbows on the way, perched on bar stools, draining their cups, fading but still trying to blend in with our French Canadian compatriots.

Angie:	Bonjooer Michele? Voolay voo voo?
Debbie:	Christ Angie, it's Vwwwooleh, not voolay!
Me:	Good night, bonsoir, good night…

AFTER A NIGHT OF FRENCH LAVENDER INFUSED SLUMBER, MORNING in the Clarendon's restaurant came as a shock.

Seated at a table for ten minutes without any service, we watched as the server who was clearly responsible for our section, passed us without so much as a nod of acknowledgement. Rainbows were scattered about, I went to Debbie's table to see how others were faring.

Me:	How's the service been?
Debbie:	Lousy.
Me:	Yeah, he's walked by our table twice without stopping.
Trudy:	He wouldn't take our order in English. Debbie had to give it to him in French.
Me:	What! You're kidding?
Trudy:	No I'm not. He's been totally obnoxious.
Me:	Well, maybe we need to complain?
Debbie:	I don't think that'll help.
Me:	Why not?
Debbie:	You'll have to ask Angie.

I looked around, but Angie was not in the restaurant.

Me:	Okay, so what happened?
Debbie:	Well, apparently, she was feeling pretty good when she got back this morning. Since the sun was coming up she decided to serenade the hotel with her rendition of Frere Jacques.
Me:	What?
Trudy:	Yep. She stuck her head out her courtyard window and sang at the top of her lungs. She woke up the whole hotel, including me.
Debbie:	And me. The manager had to shut her down. She's lucky she wasn't kicked out of the hotel.
Trudy:	She's lucky she's still alive.

I went back to our table where the server was waiting to take my order. I pointed to a line on the French only menu and said in my best accent, 'Merci'.

Part 2 - Grand-Mere, Quebec, August, 1991

Slo-Pitch National Slo-Pitch Championships

I WAS ON DECK, SWINGING MY FAVOURITE ROYAL BLUE 28 OUNCER bat at phantom balls, trying to visualize a perfect hit. But the scene around me was overpowering. Hundreds of people milling around a ball park practically big enough for the major leagues, tall bleachers around the diamond filled with hundreds of fans. A viewing tower for the local sports reporters and the game commentator who was actually calling the names of the batters and making sporadic and not always accurate comments which were hard to understand on the loudspeakers but nevertheless, in my mind, elevated the event into fantasy territory.

My childhood dream of growing up to become a professional ball player looked like this:

Me, smiling and running and throwing a ball (feet barely touching the ground) across an infinite field of green grass under a cloudless blue sky wearing a bright white uniform.

Me, in the batter's box in my bright white uniform hitting the ball into the far away stands filled with people all soaked in sunshine.

These two images together formed my fantasy and, despite my hideous kelly green ball pants and dubious throwing record, I was in fantasyland. I discovered in Grand-Mere, Quebec, that childhood dreams don't die. They just retreat into some obscure regions of our brain and wait to be activated.

This was, after all, the first ever national slo-pitch tournament in Canada. And I was there! And the guy had just called my name! I was up to bat!

I stepped into the batter's box and tried to look cool and composed, but in my head *he just said my name he announced my name I'm playing in a national tournament where names are announced and people are watching and this feels like my childhood fantasy except for these ugly kelly green pants this is a dream come true oh my god oh my god oh my god*

UMPIRE: STTTRRRRRIIIIKE ONE!

I stepped out of the batter's box and glanced at the umpire with that look that says "Seriously? Maybe you should have your eyes checked." However, in my excitement, I hadn't actually *seen* the ball.

I took a deep breath and scanned the field and sky. The conditions were ideal for a ball game – high thin cloud blocked the late day sun and the temperature warm but not hot. No wind. The four fielders equally distributed from left through centre and right field.

I stepped back into the box, raised my bat, dug my feet into the ground, and bent my body into the ready position. The pitcher dropped in a high deep shot landing well beyond my strike zone. I stayed in the box, spied the rover moving right, leaving an opening up the middle. The next pitch was mine. I sent a line drive over second base and took off for first.

Safe at first. Not a home run but I was on base. My body quivered with the utter delight of living what I knew to be the closest thing I would ever come to that childhood dream.

And that emotion, that sensation, of a dream made manifest in real time, real flesh, real air and sky, feet in cleats bat in hand, ball smacking glove, well, this was satisfaction, this was pleasure, this was validation, rejuvenation, reclamation, of my very soul.

Right there on first base, I could have stood and cried.

Right. Back to the game. This is really happening. I need to pay attention.

Part 3

PERHAPS IT WAS THE SIGNIFICANCE OF THE OCCASION, OR RAW FEAR of humiliation before so many onlookers, but my throwing problem disappeared for the duration of the tournament. Yes, for the *entire* duration of the tournament, my arm and hand and mind lined up straight. Straight enough that when, at the tournament's All Star exhibition game, played under a night sky and teeth whitening flood lights, the team sent me in to represent the Rainbows because the rest of them had already consumed a few Molson Canadians. Unknowingly, they delivered me into a celestial experience. When the one, deep, deep, high, high fly ball, so high the ball disappeared for a moment causing me to panic as I searched the sky for it out there all alone miles away from the other fielders none of whom I knew, I found it, got under it, jogged sideways, caught the ball and threw it in straight and true.

Later, at the big tournament party, I swayed under the starlight as a Newfoundlander took to the microphone to share a story in song of stormy seas and lost boats and unrequited love. At least I think that's what he was singing about. I imagined it, I visualized it, between flashbacks of that big fly ball and my big throw home.

In the months and years after Grand-Mere, I never shared with my team the truth of the Quebec Tour: I had lived my childhood fantasy. I couldn't have articulated the experience. Since Grand-Mere, I have been chasing every other dream I ever had and coming up with new ones. I have discovered that developing and maintaining a huge bank of dreams guarantees that a decent percentage will convert to reality. Just yesterday, for example, I dreamed of napping in a bath, and sure enough, there I was at 5:00 p.m., immersed in the real liquid warmth of my dream…dreaming.

CHAPTER 28

LIKE MOST RECREATIONAL ATHLETES, BALL PLAYERS OCCASIONALLY get inebriated after a game and frequently at weekend tournaments. Everyone knows about ball players getting the gravel rash. All around Canada, recreational sports leagues, especially ball leagues, are known as Beer Leagues. Beer Leagues allow players to run the bases and then later, measure them upside down. Getting ossified and afflicted is for some a rite of passage into the sport of ball.

The truth in this cannot be denied. Who has not seen a bunch of nylon pant clad women with their main braces well spliced in the local pub or in the sports field parking lot? Full of bug juice, they might be sprawled around a table or a cooler on the tailgate of a truck, tanking up. While recreational athletes love their game, they love the post-game benders just as much and most have been plastered, blasted, or screwed on booze at least once. Except, in the case of the Rainbows, Mary. Mary was never caught with more sail than ballast.

The cause of the plastering and polluting is the social aspect of recreational sport. Getting socially slammed, smashed, or shit faced is equal in importance to the sport itself because most recreational athletes have day jobs and many have kids as well. For these Canadians, their sport is their outlet, and getting a shine on one night of the week allows them to unwind. People are unwinding all over the country not only in sports leagues but in chess clubs, quilting clubs, hiking clubs, book clubs. In fact, I know a few book clubbers who regularly get crapulent and I bet some of those quilters get as tight as their stitches.

I wonder though, how many teetotalers know the real stats on stewed ball players. My observations indicate a minority of players are true liquor pigs. What's more, those hard hitters at the pub are often the hardest hitters on the field.

This was certainly the case with the Rainbows, only five of whom I have categorized as frequently liquored up. The fact that most of them were also star players who often made some of their best plays with a hangover is due to two factors. First, they had oodles of natural athletic talent. Second, they feared pissing off Mary, who became the Rainbows coach when the team had worn out Debbie and all the volunteer husbands.

A disapproving look from Mary was all it took for a hungover Rainbow to quit feeling sorry for herself and step up. When a hungover Rainbow arrived at the morning game complaining of a headache and then missed a play or struck out, they risked one of Mary's lethal looks - a mix of disgust, contempt, and plain pissed off.

Equally distressing for a hungover Rainbow was an upset Ozzie. Ozzie was Mary's husband. Ozzie did not like to see Mary pissed off. When Mary was pissed off, Ozzie's cheery face and round watery eyes would droop and he'd look like a small child attending the funeral of the family pet. "Geez you guys', Ozzie would whisper, 'Mary's pretty mad. You ought to take the game more seriously."

In reviewing the drinking habits of 20 Rainbows, I concluded that eleven players formed the responsible, safety conscious, and sober, bulk of the team. They were average to above average players. There were 4 players who occasionally became obfuscated, and only 5 who frequently pissed Mary off. These five players did, on occasion, become public nuisances, beheading motel marigolds, dislodging strings of patio lights, and falling off bar stools. However, more often they simply assaulted the ears of karaoke bar patrons and left large tips for the servers who put up with them. They were also top notch ball players. Most of the time.

CHAPTER 29

AFTER YEARNING FOR YEARS TO GET OUT OF RIGHT FIELD, IT HAS become apparent to me that right field is where I belong. In fact, I believe I was born there, but my mother insists she delivered me in a hospital maternity ward.

Although my ball team retired in 2001, I have remained in the right field of life.

The view from right field is enormous. As long as you go deep, the entire field of play can be seen at once. I can watch all the moves, all the plays, in real time. I often feel the play that's coming. I feel it on my skin and in my chest and stomach and sometimes even in my throat and cheekbones. Standing so far out, there is nothing to do but watch what's happening and, depending on the play, pray, or wish I was there. When the situation is one that calls for prayer I'm grateful I'm way out there in right field where I have no control and therefore no responsibility but still, sometimes it makes me feel sick. Like when I once watched Angie run the bases in the wrong direction, when, in life's right field, you see someone you count on go in the wrong direction, it unnerves you. If it happens in a crucial game it terrifies.

Sometimes the view from right field is too enormous. Sometimes I have to close my eyes.

But when everyone's making great plays and hitting the ball out of the park, those free falling images and thoughts flow through and effortlessly I float along and feel I am in perfect harmony with the grass, the sky, the air, the insects and critters and dust. And I can feel how such series of plays has changed me.

I feel more substantial, yet lighter. This feeling lasts days, sometimes weeks, and leaves a bright spot inside me which eventually melds with and enriches that inner luminosity that guides me from day to day, year to year.

The view from right field is that enormous.

There's a lot of down time in right field too. Time to think. To reflect. To contemplate all the day to day, year to year conundrums and confusions of life. After a few decades of reflection and contemplation, I have found more often than not that the confusions and conundrums have entered the realm of mystery. It remains a mystery to me, for example, that I still don't understand how computer technology works. I have asked many experts to explain it to me, but I am still confused and have given up my search for comprehension. I am now completely at peace when my computer does not do what I want it to do and completely in awe when it does. The same goes for marriage.

This sense of peace and awe is powerful. I have contemplated it a lot out in right field, where the sky stretches to an infinite horizon and I know it's infinite because I've been to places like Cape Spear, Canada, and Byron Bay, Australia, and there really is no end to it. Under the sky are forests and mountains and coral reefs and tidal rivers and grandchildren and the scent of lilies and the taste of artisan ice cream. These things are all mysteries to me and I hope they stay that way because I don't need to understand everything anymore. I've become fond of peace and awe.

Jealousy, greed and hatred are also awesome mysteries but since they don't generate a sense of peace when I see them I try not to let them get into me too deep. If I feel them inside me I go further out in the field to take myself out of the play. I may be all alone out there and afraid a ball might make it to me anyway, but at least I will see it coming.

I used to feel lonely in right field. Lonely and abandoned and even at times, unloved. Or unlovable? It takes time to understand those kinds of feelings, but, once you accept the position to which you've been delegated, you realize you have all the time you need to seek that understanding. Right field is full of empty quiet space in which to listen to your heart.

Getting this far while in right field has allowed me to discover I'm not alone out here. Not at all. Here, I have learned, can be seen and heard the echoes and trails of the many others who have gone before me. And too can be seen and heard the press and shouts of those coming who have yet to accept their destiny.

The view from right field is that enormous.

CHAPTER 30

LIKE A BAD CASE OF GASTROENTERITIS, OR PSYCHOGENIC HYPO-chondria, playing tricks on people and breaking the law has a way of coming back to haunt us.

During the Quebec Tour I was tricked into performing a sit-up while blindfolded. Apparently, this is a common locker room initiation trick in men's hockey that results in the rookie sitting up and planting his face squarely into one of his teammate's bare bottom. Imagine these guys, if you will. There they are, out on the ice, playing tough and strong and fast like the real men they believe themselves to be, and then later, there they are sticking their bums in their teammate's faces. Hmmm.

Fortunately, in my moment of humiliation, when I opened my eyes there was no bare skin but hovering above my face was a rather large Wrangler wrapped derriere that belonged to a Husband modest enough to not only keep his pants on but also keep a respectable distance from me, the victim. The embarrassment of the moment passed quickly as the Rainbows, all of whom, with husbands, were splayed around the hotel room with a couple of styrofoam coolers of Molson's, felt my pain and rescued me.

Debbie's husband Brian was identified as the mastermind behind the trick. Despite his notoriety for his locker room schemes and telephone calls impersonating various characters in distress, he didn't recognize the trap being set for him when Husband, who was with him when he got a parking ticket, suggested that since we were just days away from returning to the Wild West he shouldn't bother to pay the fine.

Husband slipped the ticket into his wallet where it remained until, back on our acreage, he pulled it out, placed it on the kitchen counter, and said, 'you might be able to do something with this'. At the moment I couldn't imagine what use it would be but I attached the parking ticket on the fridge with a magnet anyway.

Summer ended. The big yellow school bus came back to take my sons to school, my daughter and I spent mornings walking, picking fall flowers, singing, dancing, and drawing. During the evenings, after I had lovingly tucked all three into their beds, made school lunches for my sons and addressed the most pressing mail and school business, I descended into my dungeon where I was, that winter, studying Comparative Politics.

One afternoon during Mia's nap, I was assembling a giant batch of cabbage rolls and contemplating the previous evening's revelation that politicians of the 18th century had extended the right to vote to certain regular folk strictly as a means of garnering more power. Not to give power to the people, as I had always assumed. I was enjoying the irony of this bit of history when the idea struck.

Impersonating a lawyer, I would send a registered letter to Brian explaining I had been retained by the Quebec government to recover unpaid parking fines from out of province offenders like him.

My past career as a paralegal gave me all the resources I needed, including my friend, Sharon, an Irish Canadian troublemaker and fearless paralegal.

Me:	Sharon, it's Michele. I have a favour to ask.
Sharon:	Anything for you, woman. What's up?
Me:	I'm planning to play a little joke on someone.
Sharon:	Ooohh, I like the sounds of this already.
Me:	Can you pretend to be a lawyer for me?

Sharon: Of course. I was just admitted to the bar, didn't you know?

I drafted a letter to Brian from Sharon ---, Barrister and Solicitor, who had a contract with the Alberta government to collect the aforesaid parking tickets. The letter stated that a payment, by way of certified cheque, was required to be made, within 7 days, to Sharon, who would be collecting it on behalf of the government. The amount, $125.00, represented the original $25 fine, a $50 late payment penalty, and $75 for the legal services required to collect the fine.

Apparently, the very day Brian received the letter he called Sharon, who then called me.

Sharon: Michele, you won't believe this, Brian called today and left a panicky message on my machine. He was sorry he hadn't paid the ticket, he knew he should have paid it before he left Quebec, he said he wanted to come to my office and pay it right away, tonight!
Me: Oh no, tell him to mail it!
Sharon: What! And miss the chance to meet him in person?

Later that night, my phone rang…

Sharon: I think he's here, he's pulling up right now, he's getting out of a truck… yes, it must be him. He's crossing the street, he's coming straight toward my door, I'm going to put the phone down now…

I heard her door bell ring, her door open, and…

Sharon:	Can I help you?
Brian:	Are you Sharon ----?
Sharon:	Yes, you must be Brian.
Brian:	Yes, that's me, the numbskull who didn't pay the $25 dollar ticket that's' turned into $125.00 bucks.

After Brian poured his heart out to Sharon I heard the door close and the phone being moved....

Sharon:	Holy shit, did you hear that Michele?
Me:	Yes! Every word! And you know what? We're going to finish this joke off with such a bang. You shall be my guest at the Rainbows annual windup banquet.

AUTUMN LEAVES SWIRL INSIDE AS THE DOOR LEADING DOWN INTO the basement of the Okotoks Masonic Hall squeals opens and slams shut. From my strategically chosen seat at the back of the hall, I watch for Sharon.

When she and her husband finally arrive I don't recognize her until she slips into a chair beside me. As planned, she has disguised herself. Her strawberry blonde hair is now long and black and her large tinted glasses disguise her sparkly blue eyes. She has been transformed from professional lawyer to proper vixen.

Over the racket of dozens of friends laughing and talking and dishes banging in the kitchen, we sit at our table and go over our plan.

Dinner is served, eaten, and cleared away, and Debbie is now at the podium.

Debbie:	Okay, it's time to get the festivities going, so get your drinks topped up and do whatever else you need to do and be back in your seats in ten.

I go to Debbie and tell her to follow me to a private corner.

Debbie:	Jesus Christ, is there something wrong?
Me:	Not at all. I have a surprise for Brian. I'd like to give it to him before the regular awards start.
Debbie:	What! What's going on? Has this got anything to do with that parking ticket?
Me:	Take a look.

I pull the parking ticket and Brian's cheque out of a bag, now both neatly displayed behind glass in a frame with the words cut out and attached underneath, 'Lest We Forget'.

Debbie:	Oh my God. You mean the whole thing was a set up? Jesus Christ, Brian has been freaking out for weeks.

Debbie and I stand at the podium, someone else whistles, and the room quiets.

Debbie:	Before we begin our regular awards, Michele has a special announcement to make.

I invite Brian to join me at the podium. Reluctantly, he leaves his seat and shuffles up to stand beside me, hands in his jean pockets, shaking his head and muttering about his dislike for being in front of a crowd.

I begin, like all good stories do, with the beginning, weaving through the highlights of the Quebec Tour that led to the locker room sit-up episode, and smoothly moving on to the unfair parking ticket that Brian had decided not to pay. As he concentrates on my words, he looks at Debbie, at the other husbands, shrugs his shoulders, then drops his head down again to listen more carefully, as if there is something between the lines he needs to hear…

Somewhere around the 8th stanza, lights begin to go on in the audience. Giggles and whispers, then laughter begins to fill the room, while Brian remains confused and in the dark.

Sharon is now walking toward us, her heels reverberating on the old wood floor. When she stands and removes her wig and glasses the laughter in the room hits the ceiling.

Only Sharon and I hear Brian whisper, 'holy shit'.

This feat of subterfuge kept me warm throughout the winter that followed. In future years, when my throwing problem returned, I held on to the memory as proof that I could at times be at the top of my game.

CHAPTER 31

THE YEAR AFTER THE QUEBEC TOUR WE WENT ON OUR SECOND National Slo-Pitch Championships Tour. SPN and Molson's were being true to their commitment to make their program national. We were heading this time to the sunny prairie city of Saskatoon, Saskatchewan. Being only one province over and sharing many landscape and cultural similarities, our Saskatchewan tour was shorter and did not require any pre-tour language training. Furthermore, we had all picked, at home, the Saskatoon berries for which the city of Saskatoon is named, and so, we were content with a Best Western hotel room and restaurant that served bacon and eggs. Numerous Husbands, primarily the farmer types, joined us on the tour to take a look at the local tractors and crops.

Saskatoon, to the outsider, is a rather unremarkable prairie city. Dominated by descendants of the temperance movement who established the town in 1882 as a response to the liquor trade raging across Canada's prairies, it seemed a rather sober place. There was a sense of restraint, of moderation, in the local pubs, where no one, Rainbows or locals, were falling off bar stools, or even dancing. I don't recall any dancing in Saskatoon. We were a subdued lot, and I couldn't help but wonder if there was a hidden city within this city, where the action really was. Were the remnants of the temperance movement still in play, keeping a lid on things?

Like the tour itself, the Rainbows' performance during the national tournament was unremarkable. It was a comment of Sheila's that actually made the tour worthwhile.

We had arrived at the ball park on opening day and were approaching the registration area, which was swarming with people. Out of Sheila's gum snapping mouth came the following:

Sheila: Holy shit, look at this place, it's crawling with dykes on spikes.

Dykes on Spikes. In this year of 2018, I believe the LGBTQ community would appreciate the humour, but back in 1992, public discourse on sexual orientation was not what it is today. In fact, in 1992 in Calgary, the first Pride Parade had just occurred, but few, if any politicians joined in and the participants felt compelled to wear paper bags over their heads for fear of being recognized and subsequently being discriminated against by friends, family, and employers.

The fact that many members of the LGBTQ community were just beginning to come out in Alberta back in the early 90's did lead to some colourful commentary within social groups like the Rainbows. With Chevy Chase and Eddie Murphy including the subject in their infamous stand ups, opportunities were ripe for jokes, innuendo, and speculation, giving the everyday unenlightened masses like the Rainbows license to laugh. At the same time, we were all learning, whether we liked it or not, about the real pain many LGBTQ's suffered.

There is great irony in the fact that some heterosexual female ball players felt discriminated against because the common thinking at the time was that most female ball players were, in fact, 'dykes on spikes'. If a woman chose to play ball, chances were she had a little extra testosterone; she likely had to shave a little more than the average woman, and even if she was married with children, she really did prefer the company of women.

I don't think the Rainbows would deny there were days they preferred the company of each other over that of their husbands. Women often do have a lot more in common with other women than with men. The same goes for men, who have never felt compelled to explain their men only clubs. (Just consider what we know about their locker room games.)

Today, signs of the new era of inclusivity are everywhere. Public schools are sorting out which washroom a transgender child should use. City Mayors across Canada are now at the front of Pride Parades. Marriage within the gay community is legal and commonplace. The very subject of sexual orientation is passé, which is good news for us all.

However, In the Rainbow days, conversations about sexual orientation were hushed and still generated a certain controversy. The starter would be, "Is she or isn't she?" First consideration was appearance. If she had the look of a lesbian, she probably was one. The 'look', of course, was a perception, and could include characteristics such as extremely short hair, tattoos, and the wearing of 'masculine' clothing such as black running shoes or baggy jeans. Next, the consideration of life style. Did she hang out with women most of the time? Was she always single? If the answers to these questions were affirmative, rumours would be shared, or invented, and by the time the subject of the poor girl's private life was dropped, the air would be ripe enough to attract at least a million fruit flies.

Today, with even school boards talking in acronyms like LGBTQ, and news stories about gender reassignment surgery, a woman who happens to be wearing black sneakers and hardy grey work pants while sporting a mohawk wouldn't turn a single head. But back in the 80's, if she didn't also paint her finger and toenails pink, refrain from swearing in front of men, and hold her cigarette like a lady, she was suspect.

For those who are curious about how female ball players, straight and queer, managed the matter of their public appearance back in the 80's, here is the definitive dress code to which, if one wanted to be seen as straight, one referred. In order to avoid labelling, a minimum number of 3 of the following real girl indicators were required:

Three of these fundamentals would usually stop tongues wagging. When the Rainbows travelled to competitive tournaments, our tongues indeed wagged, but mostly with phrases like, 'Jesus Christ, look at the size of those women. We're gonna be crushed'.

The Rainbows all adhered to three or more of the above criteria. Every one of us was married or toted a boyfriend. None of the smokers on the team held their cigarette between their thumb and forefinger, but few were averse to swearing in front of men. Some of us wore our makeup at games, while others only painted up for special occasions. I don't remember seeing much cleavage but we were usually in our ball shirts or a button up western for the dances. If there was indeed a Rainbow lesbian, she was playing her game in an era when she didn't feel she could reveal herself, not even to us. This is a comment on the era, not on sexual orientation or women who played ball.

Times do change and that's often a good thing.

BACK IN SASKATOON, THE RAINBOWS WERE UNABLE TO CONVERT Sheila's limitless humour and commentary into RBIs (runs home). Our game scores were dismal, and so was our mood. Perhaps the international flavor of Montreal had spoiled us. Or perhaps we were in need of new blood. Or perhaps we were all riding the cotton pony? Were we, girls?

CHAPTER 31

Susan joined the Rainbows long after all the men who had attempted to coach us had given up. This was a good thing because had any man attempted to tell Susan how to improve her game, the first thing they would have told her was to quit laughing so much, especially when she was running to first base. For Susan to stop laughing would be as tragic as the sun to stop shining, because Susan's star quality was her ability to laugh at the world, and herself.

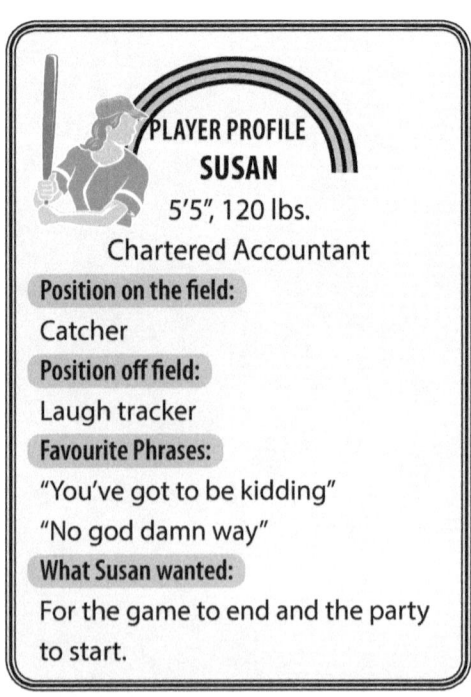

PLAYER PROFILE
SUSAN
5'5", 120 lbs.
Chartered Accountant

Position on the field:
Catcher

Position off field:
Laugh tracker

Favourite Phrases:
"You've got to be kidding"
"No god damn way"

What Susan wanted:
For the game to end and the party to start.

When Susan saw that we were up against a team of women significantly larger than us, her standard comment was:

Susan: You've got to be kidding. No god damn way am I getting near one of those Amazons.

But then she would have a few laughs and do her job, fearlessly. Crouching her slim body down behind home plate, she hung on to her position as a series of bulldozer bodies came along, cranking out deep fly balls that gave them time to lumber through the first two bases. When, half way through a game it was evident we could beat them with our speed and agility and by keeping our hits on the ground, Susan was delighted.

Susan: Christ, they can't run and they can't bend over, all we have to do is catch their flies.
Kathy: I'm not worried about beating them. I'm worried about one of them landing on you and flattening you into a pancake.

But Susan's fearlessness did not interfere with her survival instinct. She was courageous at home plate in the face of an amazon player bearing down on her, but was never foolish enough to get in the way. She came away from such games unscathed, long black hair and nails intact, the lightning in her eyes flashing with anticipation.

Susan: It's time for a drink! Let's go.

Although Tannis became a Rainbow just a few years before the team retired, her contribution was significant. Not only was she a reliable, dedicated, and enthusiastic second baser, she also served as the Rainbows vent for all matters requiring serious cursing.

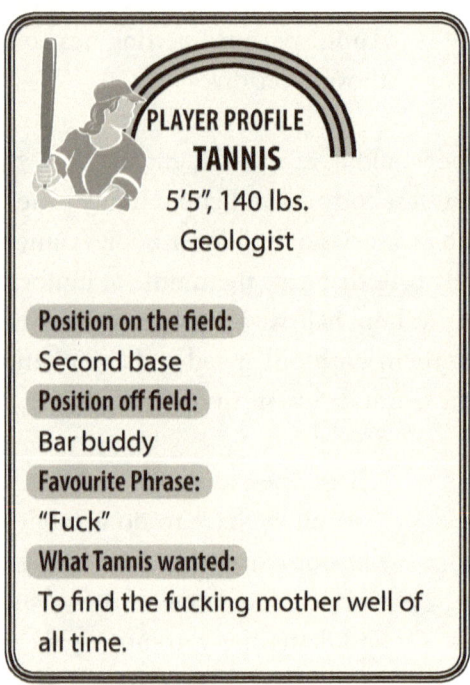

PLAYER PROFILE
TANNIS
5'5", 140 lbs.
Geologist

Position on the field:
Second base
Position off field:
Bar buddy
Favourite Phrase:
"Fuck"
What Tannis wanted:
To find the fucking mother well of all time.

A rough calculation of the number of games Tannis played as a Rainbow would be 80 (yes, I'm ball parking it.) At each game and post-game pub breakout session, she applied her favourite word on average 100X per hour. Each game/pub night lasted approximately 4 hours, which means Tannis uttered this word 400 times or more on any given night. With approximately 80 regular season games in her Rainbows career, this means her favourite word was expressed 32,000 times, or, 6,400 times per season.

Then there were the tournaments.

Since Tannis was a talented and ambitious geologist playing with the big boys in Calgary's oil and gas game, I attributed her affection for the F bomb to the stresses of her job. I never asked her husband if she eventually exhausted her pool of fucks before going to bed at night, but if she didn't, I imagine he might have found it to be to his advantage.

ONE OF THE RAINBOW'S LAST RECRUITS BEFORE THE TEAM RETIRED, Janet's relatively short career with the Rainbows was not light on impact. Her sunny and serene disposition, with a hint of detachment and mild amusement, but never condescension, in her eyes, was a reflection of her incredible poise and sense of life balance.

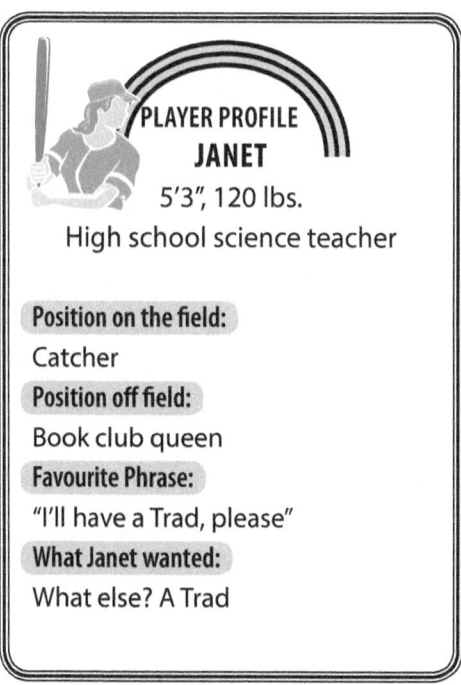

PLAYER PROFILE
JANET
5'3", 120 lbs.
High school science teacher

Position on the field:
Catcher
Position off field:
Book club queen
Favourite Phrase:
"I'll have a Trad, please"
What Janet wanted:
What else? A Trad

As Debbie had invited Janet to join the team, she had no one but herself to blame for the distraction to which Janet's detachment drove her.

Debbie: I don't know why it drives me so crazy! You should have seen me last night when I got off the phone with her. (Janet had called to say she had to miss the game that week due to a family reunion). I had an absolute hissy fit!

Hissy fits were exclusive to Debbie. Others on the team may have had conniptions, temper tantrums, or bursts of testiness, but only Debbie had hissy fits, often brought on by a player's insufficient expression of regret when they had to miss a game. A family reunion may not be a funeral, but she could accept Janet's decision to go if only she spared her the details about the wonderful family members who would be there, all gathered at the family cabin where they had been gathering every year since before Janet was born.

Other reasons for missing a game were inexcusable. For example, book clubs. It was a mystery to Debbie why Janet would choose a book club meeting over a ball game. It was over a beer at the end of the first day of play at a weekend tournament that Janet announced to the team that she would not be coming to the Sunday morning game due to her book club meeting. Being even keeled and infuriatingly independent, Janet did not feel compelled to explain further. Or even lie. This left Debbie so speechless her hissy fit was delayed until the shock subsided. All these admirable qualities, the kind so lacking in so many of our leaders today, produced for Janet a grudging respect from the team and therefore Janet was not directly subjected to the team's ridicule about her book club. However, the book club incident did forever give the team a default excuse for any Rainbow error, weakness, or failure.

Tannis: (When her latest core report came in as a dud) Fuck, I'd probably do better joining a fucking book club.

Kathy: (When she learned of Sherry's pregnancy) Maybe Janet's Book Club could recommend a read on how to prevent that problem.

Angie: (When she gained two pounds in a week.) For shit sakes, maybe if I joined a Book Club I would lose this damn cougar belly. Reading is bloody hard work, plus, you can't drink beer and read at the same time, so I should ask Janet to lend me her biggest book…

When such comments were made around a pub table after a game, Janet was oblivious. Rather than ruminate over any errors during the game, she focused on the task at hand—enjoying her Big Rock Traditional Ale. Rarely having more than one or two, when the glass arrived she adopted the demeanor of a true connoisseur, pausing to appreciate the colour before dedicating all her senses to the experience of the first mouthful, partaking of each sip of the froth topped copper brown elixir with slow and focused pleasure. Unlike an uncouth ale guzzling pub bum, Janet did not, when she returned from her brief visit to Planet Trad, smack her lips, burp, or even produce one of those long 'ahhhhhhhhs' that can reveal so much about a person. She simply opened her eyes, smiled, and quietly murmured, 'mmmm, that's good.'

CHAPTER 31

THE LAST OF THE CHRISTMAS COOKIES AND CARROT PUDDING HAD been eaten when southern Alberta settled into a classic prairie cold snap. My sons were back on the big yellow school bus, which I followed to their school at least a couple of days a week for my volunteer roles there. Yugoslavia was having a violent breakup, resulting in refugees arriving in Canadian cities like Calgary, which gave me the opportunity to volunteer as a teacher of English to foreign born adults, some of whom came with PHD's. With my daughter in ballet and playschool, and letters to the editor to be written, my days were full. As were my evenings, which that winter I spent with French voyageurs paddling rapids on their way to Hudson's Bay, where they would track down rum and guns at the nearest Hudson's Bay Trading Post. As I had at one time in my childhood lived along the Alaska Highway in a northern community originally established as a trading post, this aspect of Canadian History had profound meaning for me, and so, I was at the same time attempting some creative writing, another childhood pursuit I believed I would return to one day. That winter, midnight after midnight, I sat alone in a dimly lit living room, waiting in vain for something brilliant to appear on the page.

But none of these enthralling occupations could prevent me from dwelling on the fact that come July, I would turn 30 years old.

I was not feeling happy about that upcoming life altering event. Which does not explain why I decided to use my six and half minutes per day of spare time to paint Josh's bedroom.

This was a mistake on two fronts. First, Josh was silently envisioning the dozens of nails he would bang into his freshly painted walls in order to display his vast collection of caps. Had he only shared this vision with me in advance. Second, I hated painting. Truly hated it. Rolling paint up and down a wall without hitting the ceiling is something that should only be done by someone with two good eyes. Since I have only one, when I paint I feel half blindfolded. As the roller gets closer and closer to the ceiling, I have to slow down and squint in order to avoid painting the ceiling. As a result, the line left at the top of the wall looks like a rendering of uneven Lego blocks. Of course, taping off the ceiling is the obvious solution to this problem, but who wants to spend time taping?

Maybe that is why, like the weather, I snapped.

Me: Why did I ever start this project?? The ceiling's a mess and Josh hasn't been able to sleep in his room for a week!
Husband: You're almost finished Michele.
Me: Yes but it's 30 below outside and I can't open the window to air out the room, so who knows when the room will be livable?

I blamed my tantrum on the fact that I would be turning 30 and was disappointed that lifelong dreams had yet to be realized. That winter, they seemed so far beyond reach I was at risk of giving them up all together. Progress on my university degree was moving at a glacial pace. Despite midnight vigils, I had not produced a single piece of creative writing. And, I was still stuck in right field.

But, there was one other lifelong dream that might be achieved before turning 30. If I could not write, if I could not yet wave to the world a university credential and if I still could not claim the position of shortstop, could I not, at least, take my first trip to a tropical destination?

As I attempted to remove the smears of paint from Josh's bedroom ceiling, I made a decision. That winter, I had to go to Mexico.

Me:	What do you think about going to Mexico for a week? My 30th is coming up this summer and I have yet to go to a tropical country. In fact, I've never been east of Kindersley, Saskatchewan or south of Albuquerque, New Mexico. Let's go to Mexico!
Husband:	What? Mexico? What do you want to go there for?
Me:	Well, it's the closest tropical destination, and cheap too. Wouldn't it be fun to go for a beach vacation?
Husband:	I'm not much for beaches.
Me:	But you love to swim.
Husband:	Where are we supposed to get the money for this?
Me:	From our bank account.
Husband:	I'm not crazy about the idea.
Me:	Well, at least think about it.

A few days later...

Me:	So, have you thought any more about Mexico?
Husband:	(Laughter). No.
Me:	Come on, I've never been anywhere tropical in my life.
Husband:	It's not in the budget.
Me:	Mexico is cheap.
Husband:	Silence.

Me:	There's these all-inclusives. $650.00 per person includes the flight and a week in a hotel.
Husband:	Silence.

Love and marriage, according to various popular entertainers, is a dance that will either, a) lead the lovebirds to la la land – matching rocking chairs on a porch with a view, or, b) lead the flightless lovebirds right over a cliff, at the bottom of which, broken and bruised, they each drag their smashed bent bodies and souls in different directions.

That winter, I was dancing solo and flying south.

Me:	I really really want to go to Mexico! I can't turn 30 without having gone to one place in the world outside Canada and the United States!
Husband:	We don't have the money.
Me:	Yes we do!
Husband:	Silence.
Me:	I'm going to go. With or without you.
Husband:	(amused and smiling) You are, are you?
Me:	Yes I am. I hope you'll come, but it's up to you. I am going to see the tropics before I turn 30 if it's the last thing I do!

The impasse was finally broken on an exceptionally brutal night of temperatures dipping below -35. I was rolling on the last coat of paint when friends dropped in for a visit. They were going to book a trip to Hawaii to escape the bitter cold.

Me:	Instead of Hawaii why don't you come with us to Mexico?

Husband's eyebrows shot up.

Friends:	Never thought about going there. Why not? We should try it for a change, we always go to Hawaii. When are you going?
Me:	Soon – there's a great sale on right now, let's book it together?
Friends:	Why not! Let's do it.

Post Script:

Husband was doubtful until we walked off the hot airport tarmac and climbed into an old bus piloted by a fiesta ready senor with a cooler of ice cold cerveza at his feet. 'Only two pesos senor, hasta la vista!'

I have remained forever grateful.

CHAPTER 32

THE RAINBOWS PERFORMANCE AT THE 1993 NATIONAL SLO-PITCH Championships in Calgary does not stand out in my mind as one of our best, but it does stand out as one of my worst moments and really, looking back, I should have been benched.

It was morning, and we were in the dugout playing our first game. The sky was that white grey of impending snow. Every few years Calgary and region receives a dose of winter in the middle of summer. I don't know if this happens in other parts of Canada, but long-time residents of Calgary and area are never really surprised when a blast of arctic wind, or sleet or snow threatens their geraniums or tomato plants in the middle of August. However, that doesn't mean we don't complain about it.

Me:	I can't believe we have to play in these conditions. I can't even see the ball, it just disappears in the sky. I'm afraid I'm going to get one right in the face.
Sherry:	My hands are freezing so don't expect me to pitch strike outs.
Karen:	Fart. You know I was thinking of packing it in this year. Why didn't I listen to myself?
Debbie:	Oh for chrissakes you guys quit complaining!

That was my first signal to shut up, but....

Me:	I'm not complaining, I'm just saying this is dangerous. How am I supposed to catch flys if I can't see the ball? I'm serious. If we have to play in this weather we should at least be using a neon coloured ball.
Debbie:	Oh for shit's sakes!
Mary:	The official balls are white Michele.
Me:	Well there should be some official neon orange ones too.
Mary:	I don't think so. I've never seen any.
Me:	I'm going to go ask the umpire.

The inning hadn't started yet so I began walking out of the dugout...

Debbie:	Don't you dare. The ump'll think we're a bunch of idiots!
Kathy:	Give your head a shake Michele.
Me:	I don't care what anyone thinks, it's starting to snow now.
Kathy:	That's not snow, that's sleet, don't you know your precipitation types?
Angie:	Precipitation types, listen to you using big words...
Mary:	Angie, you're up to bat, get out there!

The sleet was brief but the cold and dirty softball coloured sky continued, as did my complaining about it. Telling your teammates you cannot see the ball does not build their confidence in your ability to carry your share of the load. Complaining about conditions either encourages others to complain or gets you benched. As I said, I should have been benched.

Although I didn't threaten to speak to the ump again about the ball colour, I fumed about it. With such extraordinary conditions,

I thought, why would an umpire not agree to the use of an orange neon ball? What was the point of inflexible official rules when players were expected to be flexible about the weather? I was not in favour of blindly following rules. And out there in right field I felt blind. And downright hard done by, damn it.

Looking back, I can see I had always resisted and questioned rules and conventions. In junior high school, I took petitions to the school principal demanding the right to wear my own gym clothes rather than the proscribed gym strip. In high school, I argued about Shakespeare with my English teacher, who thought he understood Macbeth better than I did. Meanwhile, when all the girls were wearing Adidas and Levis jeans, I was wearing three piece wool suits from Suzy Creamcheese. My favourite was a burgundy number – pencil skirt, vest and double lapel jacket. When my peers stood around at parties passing a joint, I passed it on and told them they should read *Go Ask Alice*. Instead of drinking alcohol with my high school peers, I drank it privately with my parents. I had seen too many victims of alcohol and I knew that, in order to avoid becoming one, I had to be, in public, a teetotaler. I believe the only reason many of my high school peers tolerated me in their presence was because I smoked cigarettes. Everyone had to adopt at least one cool adult like lifestyle habit.

At eighteen I drove a monster car, a 1974 Toronado, teal blue exterior with a nice trimming of rust. It never occurred to me that I would have more friends if I drove a car they wouldn't mind being seen in. I was still driving a big rusty boat when I joined the Rainbows, one that was so unconventional Angie once asked me not to park it in front of her house. She didn't want the neighbours to think it belonged to her.

At 21, instead of attending university and travelling Europe like the rest of my peers, I got married and had a baby. A strange thing to do considering I had all my life dreamed of travel, but then my brother and his wife had a baby, triggering my maternal instinct. It never occurred to me that instincts don't necessarily have to be acted on the moment they arise.

I am thankful the Rainbows also tolerated me. While the rest of the team wore their uniform with their shirts tucked in, I wore mine out. Debbie pointed this out to me a number of times to no avail. No doubt this would have been very annoying. When I began to worry about my children following in some of my more dubious footsteps, I decided I must quit smoking. In order to begin the process, I no longer kept cigarettes on me. Instead, I purchased individual cigarettes from the smokers on the team. This, no doubt, would have been particularly annoying, especially when my victim was down to their last couple of smokes.

And then there was my throwing problem. Perhaps they put up with it because of other more reliable aspects of my game, or perhaps they admired my stubborn refusal to give in. Or perhaps I was a source of amusement.

Perhaps they saw me, with all my warts, as I saw them, as an integral part of our circle of grace. That circle got us through that cold and disappointing national tour, at which we gave a dismal performance and have all agreed to forget.

CHAPTER 33

We were sharing a couple of jugs of draft and a few platters of chicken wings at Kinfolk, a new pub that had opened right across from the ball diamonds. The Lazy L era had ended with the retirement of Lester, who, I suppose, had decided he had slung enough beef carcasses and needed a change. Without any fuss, the Rainbows switched their allegiance and were now regulars at Kinfolk like all the other teams. Kinfolk was a contemporary pub that offered karaoke, which I suspect is the real reason for the switch. Angie could not get enough karaoke and, after a couple of beers, Sherry would join her, followed later by Karen, and then Debbie. It was like a communicable disease.

This foursome, like so many white women of that era, envied the black Motown R&B ladies. All over North America during the karaoke craze, in thousands of pubs, middle aged white women were trying to emulate Diana Ross and the Supremes. I wanted to talk about the Burnaby Nationals, which we were heading to later that summer. Burnaby was the place of my birth and location of some of my earliest and fondest childhood memories.

Me:	So, are any of your husbands coming to Burnaby? Mine isn't.
Debbie:	Why not? We're only going for 6 days.
Angie:	Rob has been complaining about it too. I told him I'd pack him seven pairs of underwear so he could shit himself once.
Kathy:	That's hilarious Angie…

Me:	Hey, has anyone ever been to the White Spot in BC?
Rainbow:	What's that?
Me:	It's the home of the Triple 0 Burger! They are seriously the best burgers you'll ever eat. We have to go to a White Spot when we're in Vancouver.
Mary:	Okay Michele, if you say so.
Me:	We should go to White Rock too, for fish and chips. And try out the Spaghetti Factory in Gastown. Has anyone ever been to Gastown?
Debbie:	Sounds like we're gonna be too busy on a food tour to play any ball.

It was true. My anticipation for the Burnaby tour was not for the ball games, but for my own trip down my sweetest memory lane.

I was actually dreading the games because I had discovered that psychogenic hypochondria is an incurable disease. Despite routine visualization sessions and several wondrous remissions, my psychogenic hypochondria aka throwing problem had returned and was in full force for our 1995 National Slo-Pitch Championships Tour in Burnaby. While I was a consistently reliable warm-up partner, throwing straight hard balls one after another, I was not reliably converting this performance into plays in the field. Occasionally, Kathy, who I often warmed up with, would try to cure me.

Kathy:	Christ Michele, your throws are perfect during warm up. Why don't you just tell yourself you're doing a warmup throw when we're in a game?

Debbie also tried to help.

Debbie: Brian says it's all in your head. You're just thinking too much.

Throws meant for first base went home, throws meant for home went to first base. When my play was to second, Kathy at short, Karen at third, and Angie in left all covered Tannis at second, because chances were good I would miss the mark. Every time I made a bad play I shrunk a little more in the eyes of my monstrous leprechaun, who had become so large and heavy he now had to straddle his legs around my neck and hang onto my forehead with his dry cold hands. After a bad throw he would squeeze my skull, causing me to feel dizzy, confused, and completely out of control of my senses. With false bravado I would run back to my position in preparation for the next batter, and apply what I now know to have been an astonishing wallop of denial to that leprechaun, a denial that was crucial to my survival out there in right field. Without it, I would have crawled into the nearest rodent hole and vanished. Forever.

Trying to overcome a condition such as psychogenic hypochondria is a little like trying to get a two-year-old to sit politely at the dinner table until the adults are ready to say, "Okay Susy, you may now be excused." There will be successes and of course parents must try, they must, because, eventually, Susy will turn three and then four, and then become an adult, and who wants to hang around an adult who can't remain politely at the table until everyone is done?

But two-year-olds are two, and then three, and then four, for a very very long time during which there are far more meals when they flout all the rules and refuse to eat the well balanced meal put before them and instead take off for the nearest toy.

The only sensible thing parents can do is accept that like a river, life must take its own course.

And then, capitulate.

In Burnaby, I began to ask myself if I too should capitulate.

I wondered if my condition was a form of self-sabotage. Was there some deep, deep fear within me, a fear so dangerous to my psyches it dare not be allowed to surface? And if that was in fact the case, what could possibly happen if I did indeed succeed? Would I miss a grounder and take another ball in the face and this time lose all my teeth? Would my ego be unleashed and become a monster? Would I dare to aim higher, perhaps start that professional ladies league and abandon my children?

And if any of these or other equally ridiculous scenarios were known to my sub-conscious, why wasn't it telling me?? Was I too fragile for the truth?

This constant mental battle was wearing me out. I soon began to ask myself a more practical question: was it time to give up? There was no point denying that after ten years with the Rainbows, I was no closer to shortstop than I was to that rocking chair on the porch with a view. There were things in my life that, try as I might, I could not seem to change.

But there were so many other things to be thankful for! Things I celebrated in my heart every day. My children were now 12, 10, and 7 and were my greatest joys. They embraced their lives with all the enthusiasm, confidence, and hope they would need to overcome any of their own challenges. With me as conductor, they willingly moved to the rhythm of our household and our days usually began and ended on key. As a mother I could not have been more pleased, more gratified.

I had acquired about half the credits I needed for my university degree and, although the process felt like an extreme sport, I was still in the game and hadn't run out of steam.

I had been to Mexico. Twice! I had even been to Cuba, where I ate in one of Ernest Hemingway's favourite restaurants. This, for a frustrated writer, should have inspired me. It didn't, but I could at least imagine how it might have.

Yet, there was that damn leprechaun, squeezing my skull in Burnaby. Out in right field I watched the batters hitting flies and grounders to the left side of the field and instead of calling in my mind *come to me, come to me!* I was whispering *please, don't hit my way, please. Please.*

This turn of attitude was profoundly disturbing. I should have sought therapy immediately or at least gone back to my motel room for a marathon visualization session.

Instead, I went to The White Spot for a Triple O Burger with Kennebec fries and a Fraser Valley blueberry pie.

After that I called my cousin and asked her to take me to White Rock for fish and chips.

Then I asked her to take me to my grandma's house. I wanted to see the house my beloved Ivory soap smelling grandmother had lived in until she died.

I realized, as we left White Rock, that since the Rainbows had decided to go to the Burnaby Nationals I had wanted, fiercely, to see my grandmother's house. She had died when I was eleven and my family was in the middle of the move to that place in the north that, from the moment of arrival, demanded my complete attention.

I needed to see my grandmother's house. The house with the hushed mysterious attic where gauzy light gave away nothing. The house with the cold room under the stairs filled with jars and jars of her home canned peaches and pears and cherries that came from the trees that I loved to climb in her backyard. The house where my grandfather always sat beside a big old wooden radio, clicking his false teeth.

The house which held for me the sweetest childhood memories and no sadness, no disappointment, no lost dreams.

My cousin didn't know the house—she was from the other side of my family—, but she knew her way around Burnaby and was more than happy to help me find it. I didn't have the address but when I described the hill, and told her about the playground and the old corner store and the busy road at the bottom of the hill, she knew which street to head for.

In her little economy size import we zipped in and out of traffic under a sunny blue sky, talking about her menswear retail business and what our separate lives had been like, growing up with mothers who were sisters and had their own leprechauns to contend with.

The house had just been demolished. The excavator that had done the job was still on the lot, surrounded by debris. Stunned into silence, I sat in my cousin's car feeling like I had just been punched in the gut. Feeling like something had just been violently ripped out of my arms.

It was hard to play ball after that. Really hard.

The image of my grandmother's demolished house dominated my mind in Burnaby. At the same time that I was enjoying a stroll through Stanley Park with my cousin, I was feeling this loss. Something I hadn't known was there, inside, had suddenly departed, leaving me with this sense of emptiness, this sense that I was missing something.

I was missing something.

Out in right field later, I asked myself if I should capitulate. I asked myself:

What is this all about? This wishing for the batter to go left? This throwing problem? What exactly is wrong with me? Why am I putting myself through this? Why do I still feel the pain of my grandmother's house in my heart?

Somehow I got through the tournament. While the rest of the Rainbows were, post games, taking turns on the stage of the karaoke bar near our Coquitlam motel, I was grieving my grandmother's house. I was grieving my grandmother.

The Rainbows didn't make it into the finals at the Burnaby Nationals, but we won enough games to feel like stars of that karaoke stage. While I was learning about delayed grief, a pale pink version of Diana Ross and the Supremes were outdone by their equally pale pink husbands, who surprised and delighted everyone with a brand new act called Jack and the Cracks.

Jack and the Cracks. Four Husbands who could no longer resist their inner exhibitionists. Four farmer capped red neck Alberta boys, checkered snap button shirts tucked into their dangerously low riding Wranglers, the bottoms of which were bunched up over their sneakers, presented their debut at the local Coquitlam, British Columbia karaoke bar, Summer of 95. The title song? Hello Mudda, Hello Fadda.

They were hilarious. They were a hit. They should have gone on the road.

You had to be there.

CHAPTER 34

As everyone knows, divorce nowadays is as common as white sports socks. This fact has resulted in untold numbers of middle-aged divorced Canadian and American women alone and out there in the world, wandering. They can be found on trails in jungles, mountains, rainforest, and gigantic caves, on Chinese junks and side by side in kayaks, snorkeling, whale watching, or doing the dishes in a remote HI hostel. Their most popular haunts seem to be long solitary stretches of impossibly fine sandy beaches, and airports. The airports and the beaches are the best places to find these women, in whose faces it is plainly evident that there is a continent wide identity crisis going on.

After 25 years of forming a family, a home, a professional career, and becoming highly competent in yoga or kick boxing, these women have either been cut loose or have cut themselves loose, and are now travelling around Planet Earth trying to figure out what it was all for, and what they're supposed to do now. Their faces are a series of short stories – depending on what point of their journey they are on – you may see the wide-eyed wonder and joy of a child playing for the first time in the waves of an ocean, or a Yoda like look that says, *I have the answer, there is no answer*. In airports you can find the story that says, *don't look at me here as I eat my first meal alone on this trip*, and then wander down the concourse and find another that says, *look at me all you want, I'm okay with it now*. Ideally, these women will, at the end of their journeys, return home with a renewed sense of self and purpose.

This most common of contemporary female experience has not come to the Rainbows. Very few Rainbows have had an identity crisis. In fact, virtually all of the long term players are still married to the same husband they had, or acquired, when they were a Rainbow. Compared to today's divorce statistics that say that one out of every two marriages fail, the Rainbows divorce rate stands at around one out of every six. Why? How?

Is it because they married men who simply adore them and whom they adore? While Darlene and her husband did actually dwell on Planet Adoration, it is simply impossible for me to imagine Debbie and husband, or Kerry and husband, or Karen and husband, declaring they adore each other, and, while I can imagine Angie using such language, her husband would have shaken his head and wondered what she was talking about.

No, adoration would not be the reason for so many long term stable marriages.

Nor is dependence the answer. The Rainbows were and still are fiercely independent women, creatures of the women's liberation era with its irreverence toward many of the traditional expectations of married life. They worked hard and had their own bank accounts and didn't rely on their husbands for anything other than to provide a fatherly figure to their children. Beyond that, Husbands were free to do as they pleased while always being welcomed to come along for the Rainbow ride.

And many of them did come along, regularly. At every National Tour and at many home games there was a contingent of Husband's, drinking a few Canadians or Coors Light and keeping the barbeques busy. They kept a respectful distance, never entering the player's box or approaching the bench with advice or ideas. A few were likely afraid of Sheila or Kathy who would have seen such presumption as an opportunity for a cutting remark, but that was not it, really. The Rainbows Husbands had the same respect for our team as they had for any other team of adults, men or women. We were playing our game our way, and that was enough. Being of the generation of men who saw women burn their bras, they may also have been in awe of what their wives could do. Perhaps they grew up with mothers and aunts who kept to the kitchen and garden and nursery and were still in awe that their women were out there on a ball field, playing the game as if it was the most natural thing in the world. Which of course, it was.

Let us raise a glass of beer then, to the Husbands.

CHAPTER 35

AFTER THE BURNABY NATIONAL CHAMPIONSHIPS THE RAINBOWS took a long break from national competition to concentrate on their golf games. Oh, we played ball and continued to dominate the local league, but on the bench during games the conversation was decidedly golf centric.

Kathy:	You golfing in that tournament next weekend Miller?
Debbie:	Yeah, Kerry and Wendy and Susan and I just put a foursome together for it last week.
Kathy:	Sherry and I are in. We dragged Karen out too. Should be fun.
Mary:	Oh, it'll be fun alright. There's too many players, I think.

I was appalled.

Me:	Golf is a game for old people, you guys.
Wendy:	Well Michele, we are old.
Sherry:	I'm not old yet, but I feel about ninety.
Kathy:	You look it some days too Snodgrass.

Sherry laughed and lit up a smoke.

Angie:	Don't worry Michele, we may be getting old and our knees and shoulders and just about every shittin' part of our bodies are

	falling apart, but we're still the best damn team around. I won't quit even though it's true golf is a lot easier on my knees, let me tell ya there's some mornings after ball I can barely stand up when I get out of bed, and I should probably go see the doctor….
Kathy:	Oh come on. You just need to quit eating so many pork chops. That cougar belly isn't getting any smaller.
Me:	What do you see in the game anyway? All you do is drive around in a cart, get out, take one swing, then get back in the cart. I don't get it.
Janet:	I walk.
Kathy:	Yeah, you're one of those pains in the ass that hold up the rest of us.
Angie:	Well the game can be a little boring sometimes, but it's pretty fun after in the clubhouse during Happy Hour.
Kathy:	The game is never boring with the travelling drink cart.
Me:	Exactly. That's what really keeps you going. You need a few to make things interesting.

For some Rainbows, the days of chasing national medals were over. The new goal was pain relief. Especially for knees. There were a lot of torn and worn out ligaments and ACL's and meniscuses that were preventing these Rainbows from bolting like lightning out of the batter's box. Instead, they were taking off more like thunder, starting with a low slow roll.

Worse, one of our pitchers, Darlene, had quit, leaving Sherry the sole responsibility of this key position. Being the only pitcher on a team equates to being a single parent in a household. All the children are relying on you and you alone.

Sherry had also surprised the team, and herself, by having another child. With her first two children already teenagers, it was easy for this new girl to wrap her older siblings and her parents around her little finger. She instantly became the apple of Sherry's, and the Rainbow's, collective eye. Sherry was aging as defiantly as possible and living with a chronic disease. Her new daughter ignited in her a desire to spend more time at home, playing easier games like ring around the rosy.

At our pre-season meetings, Sherry had begun to ask:

Sherry: Who else is going to pitch around here? I'm getting tired of this.
Rainbows: Not me.
Sherry: Debbie, you better find someone soon because I'm just about done.

She looked at Kathy and laughed.

Sherry: I'm tired of this outfit. And I'm tired of looking at Atkins too. You hear that Kath?
Kathy: What?
Sherry: I said I'm tired of looking at you. Like I've been telling you for years Kathy, nice legs, shame about your face.

They both laughed, their laughter rich and rising from deep within, the rest of us laughed with them, but there was that sense of something shifting. Of weariness. Of sore knees, and shoulders. And a readiness, a need perhaps, for change.

I too, had questions, the same ones that began in Burnaby when I faced my grandmother's demolished house and an empty space opened inside of me. *Where was I going? What was I going to do when the kids no longer needed me? Would I ever be able to write the stories I felt I needed to write?*

In search of an answer, when my daughter Mia entered elementary school, I tried an eclectic variety of side jobs.

I began with a volunteer stint at the local newspaper, with a weekly article similar to those in papers called Society Page. The difference was that, since DeWinton, Alberta, didn't boast any resident Nobel Prize winners, past prime ministers or senators, or even old stage stars, I didn't bother including photos in my titillating articles about our local Thanksgiving dinners, Family Dances, and Bingos. There was, actually, a rumour that K.D. Lang had moved into the biggest house in DeWinton, but she never showed up at any of DeWinton's events, not even the big annual New Year's Eve dinner and dance. Eventually, the rumour was proven to be unfounded.

While volunteering at a local college as an ESL tutor for newly arrived traumatized refugees, I began playing the trumpet. This was to satisfy my creative side and to try and keep up with my children who had all become competent musicians. However, the experiment ended abruptly when, during a public performance with the local music society I had joined, I was unable to produce a single note due to a vicious cold sore on my bottom lip. Our conductor, a rather bossy high school teacher, conveyed his disappointment with a look that suggested that if our Green band received a poor review, it would be entirely my fault.

For a few strange weeks I transcribed the confidential reports of a high profile local psychologist who was frequently quoted in radio and print. Learning of the struggles of some of his patients relieved some of the worry I felt about my own. While my midnight creative writing sessions were causing me profound frustration, at least I wasn't hearing voices that were telling me to run naked through the supermarket. If my leprechaun had tried something like that on me, I would have known for sure he wasn't real. I was fascinated with the patient stories I was transcribing and would have liked to stay on in the job, but I got tired of the constant shouting and screaming between the doctor and his secretary. Even the patients, sitting in the waiting room, knew there was something seriously dysfunctional going on, and I know one for sure who figured out the doctor was a bigger lunatic than she, and left. I wasn't far behind her.

During my identity crisis, I accidentally became famous. My local Co-op grocery store was doing a new ad campaign which involved interviews and photographs of random shoppers, like me. While I was squeezing a lemon to determine its juiciness, I was approached by a film crew and asked if I would comment on why I shopped there. This innocent exchange led to a short career in modelling and acting. For months after, my face was plastered on gigantic posters hanging from the ceiling every ten feet from one end of the Co-op store to the other. It was plastered on gigantic billboard displays at the corners of intersections around the city. It stared back at me when I flipped through Co-op flyers looking for the week's specials. I was a Co-op special.

The fame (but not fortune) of being the Co-op Lady opened doors to other opportunities. I became the face of a local realty, a local eyewear company, and even made it into a Japanese movie. Although I never did see the movie I'm pretty sure I'm famous in Japan too because I was standing right behind Japan's most beloved popular movie stars for at least ten seconds. I also learned that famous Japanese movie people prefer a burger and fries over sushi for lunch.

The Rainbows, especially Angie, desperately wanted to know the details of my modelling career.

> Angie: What's it like being famous Michele? Come on, tell us about it, we want to hear all the juicy details.

The rest of the team would look at me expectantly.

Angie: Oh come on! What's so secret about it? It must be fun, I bet you're meeting famous people, are you going to do any sexy stuff, hahahha, like those giant pictures they hang up at the lingerie shops in the malls, imagine being one of those models, I don't know if I could do that no matter how much money I could make, how much money do models make anyway?

Kathy: Yeah right, like you're gonna be a lingerie model with that cougar belly.

Inexplicably, every time the subject arose, I clammed up.

It was a shame that I was unable to talk about the modelling with the Rainbows because modelling, after all, is nothing more than a lark, an utterly trivial pursuit, an opportunity to step out of real life and play dress-up or, in my case, just fake it until you get your bearings again. A few sessions with directors and bored photographers is all it takes to find out that everyone in that business is faking it. Imagine, for example, feeling overjoyed about a trip to a science museum. Adults who go to science museums do not jump up and down and high five each other in the manner of people who have just won the biggest Lotto 649 in history. And they do not wear bright attractive clothing. They wear tattered navy khakis and old brown sweaters. They study the exhibits quietly, test the various experiments for reliability, and, if they discover something really clever, they smile. At a science museum photo shoot, a director telling the models to get into it, and look like they're having a ball, cannot be taken seriously. In the modelling business, the only people to be taken seriously are the gaffers and grips because they know how to turn the lights off and on and get in and out of the building.

So why not share my observations and have a good laugh about it with the Rainbows? Why did I feel my own strange sense of embarrassment? Was it the minor distress my little foray into fame and stardom had caused my household? Apparently, having a wife/mother become the Co-op Lady did not produce the pride one would expect. My oldest said he would have preferred if his mom's face wasn't hanging above all his friends when they went shopping with their moms at the Co-op. Husband maintained his usual silence. I therefore went about my new career stealthily, living a kind of double life. Co-op Lady by day, homework coach, chief cook, and university student by night.

Was my embarrassment tangled up with the creeping sense of disappointment I was experiencing with where I had taken my life at that point? I had begun to scold myself about not having achieved anything yet. I had no university credential, no real career, no expertise. I certainly hadn't saved the world. And I couldn't even throw a ball straight anymore.

And out in right field, my leprechaun howling with delight, I willed the batters to go left. *Go left. Go left. Go left.*

It wasn't until the spring of 2000 that a solution, an escape plan from my fake life, finally presented itself.

I became a rural municipal politician.

Municipal politics, mind you. *Rural* municipal politics. Rural municipal politics rarely requires the deception and backstabbing that we have all seen as highlights of a successful national political career. Although practiced by municipal politicians from time to time, these methods are not the main tools in a rural municipal politician's toolbox. Instead, rural municipal politicians generally use protracted consultation, finger pointing and long summer recesses to deal with difficult issues. Overall, I was a reasonable fit with my fellow elected councillors, all of whom were old men, local farmers who were there to either protect the agricultural values of the region, or to make a few extra bucks because farming isn't always that lucrative.

It's easy to become a rural municipal politician when you have dared to become a local personality by putting your face on giant posters and your opinions in writing. The voting public can identify with you. Or despise you. Fortunately, the poster images had faded, and many of my opinions were fairly mainstream. I was by then, a typical Conservative Albertan.

Although politics is a natural choice for a socially conscious and vocal citizen, if it hadn't been for a couple of neighbours who called to suggest it, the idea would never have occurred to me. By the year 2000, both sons were driving themselves to their senior high school and Mia had started rioting her way through junior high. I had my eye on the last twenty-five credits I needed to complete the longest undergraduate degree program in history. In order to figure out what exactly I should do with the damn degree once I got it, I was completing Meyers Briggs and other personal profiling tests. (I resisted having my colours done. I already knew I was a Rainbow.) After receiving the results of these tests I would argue with myself because none of them offered the answer I really needed to hear. The results did not suggest I give up my office job, my volunteer work, ball, and modelling, and take a decade long sabbatical to figure out how to write again.

Nor did the results suggest I go into politics.

The Rainbows found out I was running in my district's by-election that June by reading about it in our local newspaper.

Debbie:	I read in the Wheel you're running for Division 6.
Me:	Yeah.
Debbie:	Well, I'm not surprised. You'll be good at it.
Angie:	Hey Michele! Rob says maybe our road will finally get fixed!
Debbie:	It's not your road, Angie. You live in Okotoks, remember?
Angie:	Anyway, I bet you'll win Michele and before you know it you'll be the President of Canada!

Debbie: Oh for Chrissakes Angie! Prime Minister, not President!
Angie: Oops, right, that's right, what am I saying? Prime Minister Michele Veldhoen. That's got a real ring to it, don't you think?

Two of us ran in the district by-election. Out of less than three hundred votes cast I won by a margin of about twelve. Most people don't vote in June, it's either too nice out and they're busy with more pleasurable activities, or it's too rainy to go anywhere.

Like the modelling, I didn't want to talk about the politics with the Rainbows, but this time, it was because I didn't have a clue what I was doing. Since this condition is apparently true of a lot of politicians, I didn't feel too bad about it, but admitting it might not build confidence in my constituents, so I faked it. I also didn't know how to explain the complicated web of feelings and thoughts that had led me there. I dared to even think that finally, I had an opportunity to try and make a real difference in the world. I knew I was a good talker and wasn't afraid to ask the hard questions. But I felt nervous. Terrified, actually. What if someone saw through my mask of false bravado? What if I asked a really stupid question? What if I made one of my constituents so mad they came over to my house and shouted at me and scared my kids? Or worse, flung horse manure at my windows?

Soon after winning the election, I found out that applications for subdivisions and development permits for dugouts and accessory buildings were not exactly society altering issues with the potential to foment civil unrest or pave the way to world peace. Unless, that is, the accessory building interfered with the neighbour's view of a nearby coulee, or, much more seriously, the Rocky Mountains. Never, ever, propose to erect a building that would interfere with a neighbour's view of those mountains.

Despite the mundane nature of rural municipal political issues, after the first few months of public hearing marathons and budget sessions, I began to enjoy the job. This had less to do with the weekly lunches at which I watched my fellow councillors salivate at the sight of the local Chinese diner's version of rice pudding, and more to do with the challenge of recognizing bullshitters.

In any given year, municipal councillors sit through hundreds of public hearings during which both private and corporate citizens explain and seek approval for their applications, the majority of which, in rural areas, involve subdividing land to allow for more residential homes. While most of these applications are legitimate and acceptable, there are plenty enough that are not. This provides councillors an ideal training ground for their bullshit detectors. My own personal bullshit detector became fairly reliable and at times, went off with such ferociousness that the local news reporter felt it worthy of a story.

Angie:	Hey Michele, I read in the paper about that awful campground that the MD is finally gonna make that guy clean up. I hear the guy's been polluting the river, plus the electrical wiring in that old dance hall is really bad, it's amazing the place hasn't burned down. So what exactly did you say to him? The paper wrote that *Councilor Veldhoen* was *adamant*, about getting the campground cleaned up.
Me:	I just told him what I thought.
Angie:	I guess you can't tell me all the juicy details but what's gonna happen there now. I hear there's a bike gang that hangs around there.
Me:	I've heard that too, but I don't know if it's true. We're just trying to get him to comply with the conditions of his operating permit.

Angie:	Rob says we won't get to know everything because of those secret meetings councillors have....
Me:	They're not secret meetings Angie, they're just confidential. We go in-camera sometimes but there's still a record of the discussion.
Angie:	In-camera? You mean you take pictures of your meetings?

Out in right field, my psychogenic hypochondria was dampened by thoughts of whether or not my colleagues and I should approve the latest cell phone tower proposal or how the MD was going to pay for a new snow plough. I mused about meetings with the transportation minister who refused to pave certain roads in the MD or insisted on using death counts as a measure for whether an uncontrolled intersection was or was not safe.

What I also mused about was the fact that these thoughts were intruding on my Rainbows time. No longer were my day to day concerns being left behind with the dust as I ripped up the gravel road from home to Okotoks for ball games. In fact, that road had been paved. In bed at night, instead of visualizing good throws of the melon ball, I was visualizing debates with councilors. I began to realize, with sorrow that, like the team golfing contingent whose knees were demanding a change, so too, was my heart demanding new priorities.

CHAPTER 36

THE RAINBOWS WERE MEETING IN THE SPRING OF 2000 AT THE new Boston Pizza in Okotoks. We hadn't abandoned our regular pub, but Okotoks was growing and big chain restaurants in town were a novelty. The subject of the meeting was whether or not the team wanted to take a shot at the Provincials that year to qualify for the 2001 Nationals which were slated to take place in Newfoundland. Debbie knew the Rainbows had reached their collective pot of gold but she was looking for one last fling.

If the Rainbows played ball in Newfoundland, after all, they would be able to say they had played ball from coast to coast. Plus, who wouldn't want to play ball in Newfoundland? Who wouldn't want to just go to Newfoundland? The most easterly point in all of North America is on Newfoundland soil, and by 2000, Newfoundland's diaspora in the west had shown Albertans that Newfoundlanders were serious party people with a flair for hospitality.

Debbie:	Where the hell is everyone?
Mary:	Well, I talked to Kerry before I left the house, she said she was having some trouble with one of her cows. Apparently it gave birth to a calf with three legs.
Angie:	Three legs!? So what do they do when that happens, imagine a baby cow with three legs, how would it walk…

Mary:	If they can, they will amputate the extra leg.
Angie:	And then what do they do with the leg? Hey, maybe they could donate it to the war amps....
Debbie:	Jesus Angie!
Angie:	I know but why not? My mom had three kidneys you know, and she gave one up for adoption.
Atkins:	Janet's probably at her book club.
Debbie:	Well Jesus Christ!
Mary:	What about Sherry, Deb?
Debbie:	She can't make it. Kelly's got a game. She says she'll come to Newfoundland, but it'll be her last year. So at least we know we have a pitcher next year. But at this rate, we might not have anyone else.
Susan:	Sure we will, who wouldn't want to go to Newfoundland? It'll be a blast!

Debbie had, I believe, begun secretly maneuvering us toward the 2000 Provincials when she learned the 2001 Nationals would take place in Newfoundland. Picking up a couple of younger players with sufficiently supple knees and registering us for qualifying tournaments, she had all the bases covered for the 2000 season.

Mary:	It seems like a long ways to go for a ball tournament, but I guess it would be fun.

I was sitting at the end of a long bench along the wall, listening. Like a glove, the idea of going to Newfoundland to play in a national ball tournament fit my old childhood dreams, and my love of travel. I knew if we qualified, I would go. Yet I felt myself drifting slowly but irresistibly away from the Rainbow world toward some thing, or some place, where the Rainbows wouldn't be. I felt a sense of loss. Melancholy. For fifteen years this team, these seasonal friends, had anchored my springs and my summers. They had infused my life with riotous frivolity and inspired me with their zeal for living, their determined refusal to let life's difficulties dull the dazzling colours of that rainbow of grace we entered each time we gathered to play our game. They had been my escape from the John Deere lawn tractor, the beautiful exhausting children, the midnight vigils with blank pages, the disconnected conversations with Husband who also saw the time coming when the children would leave the nest and was imagining a world with speed boats and skidoos for fast exploration of local landscapes while I was imagining new hiking boots and a backpack for slow treks through the Rockies, the Alps, and the Himalayas.

Kerry:	I'd like to go but I don't know if Jack could handle spending three weeks down there. He'd miss Chungs too much and worry he wouldn't be able to find a good steak.
Janet:	He won't need steak, they've got the best seafood in the world. The Digby scallops are like little steaks, hmmm. And the mussels. I plan on eating a pail of mussels every day.
Tannis:	Hey, have you guys heard about the Bay of Fundy? It's fucking huge, the biggest tide in the world, there's fucking fossils like nowhere else, I've gotta see those for sure.
Susan:	Yeah, and PEI's supposed to have some great golfing.
Me:	Golfing?
Mary:	Hahaha, you might as well try it Michele, you're going to have to, sooner or later.

Debbie:	It sounds like you guys want to go then.
Me:	I have a friend from St. John's whose father still lives there and loves to give local tours. Do you want me to arrange something?
Kathy:	That depends.
Angie:	Yeah, we don't wanna get stuck with some old fart who just wants to talk history and all that stuff, I mean a little bit of history is okay but I don't wanna spend all day going through a bunch of shittin' museums or anything....
Tannis:	I can tell you one museum I'm going to in Halifax. The Alexander Keith Brewery, it's the oldest fucking brewery in Canada, they do tours.
Susan:	I'm doing that one too, we can have a few brewskies while we're there.
Me:	I'll try to find out if there will be any good concerts on while we're down there. The East Coast music scene is amazing.
Tannis:	I hope you're not talking about Rita McNeil or the Rankin Family, man, they just hurt my ears.
Me:	You should listen to Jimmy Rankin, he's fantastic but I was actually thinking more about Great Big Sea.
Debbie:	Is anyone actually thinking about the tournament?

We ate pizza and shared a pitcher or two of beer and made plans for the tournament we would have to place at in order to qualify for the Provincials. Affection for my team flooded my heart, but at the same time I felt, deep inside, relief. I would miss these times but I wouldn't miss my leprechaun. My days of the melon ball, the throwing problem, the psychogenic hypochondria were coming to an end.

Despite a few Rainbows closing in on half a century old, in 2000, we managed to become the SPN Alberta Provincial Women's Slo-Pitch Silver Medalists. This may have been the result of dropping to a lower division to which others with knackered knees had also been reduced, or it may have been because we had picked up a few younger players whose knees did not require medication to climb into the pickup and drive to the game.

Unlike the unforgettable exhilaration of Medicine Hat after winning the 1990 Provincial Championships, I don't remember the 2000 games. In fact, I don't even remember where exactly in Calgary they were. Nor do I recall a big post-victory party. Perhaps because half the team had to go home and ice their knees, while the younger half went home to walk their dogs. Being of the new generation of young women, not only were these girls unmarried and childless, they were also far more responsible than we had been at their age.

CHAPTER 37 – Part 1

NEWFOUNDLANDERS ARE THE CROWN JEWELS OF CANADA. TRULY. Not only do they staunchly and cheerfully guard Canada's most easterly point, out there in the cold wild Atlantic, they are also Canada's Kings and Queens of Hospitality. I feel reasonably safe writing these words because I have either played ball or been to a major airport or a gas station in every other province and one territory in Canada. Customer service at major airports and gas stations are definitive measures of a province's hospitality. Calgary's airport, for example, sports senior citizens in red vests and white cowboy hats who patrol the concourses looking for dazed travelers who need direction. They approach such lost and confused souls with big smiles and a friendly hand and gently guide them to their destination. Meanwhile, at Toronto's Pearson, best to transit through that airport with a full grip on your senses and a fierce sense of independence, characteristics I assume are indicative of the residents of Toronto.

Of course, there is always a flip side to everything, including regional character. And so, Newfoundlanders being Newfoundlanders, when we arrived at the Mount Pearl diamond for our first game of the 2001 National Slo-Pitch Championships, there was no one there.

Debbie:	Oh for Chrissakes, this can't be for real.
Mary:	Maybe we're at the wrong diamond?
Deb:	No, I'm sure we're at the right diamond. Unless they changed it and didn't bother to tell us.

The diamond had actual dugouts, the kind you see the professional baseball players sitting in, but not so fancy. If you watch professional baseball on T.V. you can see the players down in those dugouts, tense as guy wires in a gale, which seems to make them spit. They spit a lot, but at least it's no longer the gross brown spit from the wads of chewing tobacco they used to keep in their mouths. Now it's just water from their super deluxe personalized water bottles. But they still spit it out as if it were snuff. Of course, these dugouts wouldn't hold even the players of a professional baseball team, never mind their entourage. Dug into the ground to about thirty centimetres and lined and roofed with warped wooden boards that I imagined had come from an old fishing boat that had been lost at sea and then returned to shore in pieces ready for the wood pile. I stepped down into one and looked around. Gum wrappers, empty potato chip bags, and other bits of convenience store flotsam lined the boards of the dugout and cluttered the dirt under the bench. Seeing no cigarette butts, I concluded this dugout was used only by kids. I looked out on the diamond and noticed an actual pitcher's mound. Clearly, this diamond had been built not for softball, but for baseball. Sherry will love that, I thought. And there she was with Kathy, standing out there on the mound, laughing her head off.

Susan:	Hey Deb, there's a car coming, there's a few cars coming, looks like we're in business!
Deb:	Well it's about time.

At least twenty women, clearly the organizers, clamored out of those few cars, but it sounded more like a hundred as they swarmed the small concession stand and dugouts delivering supplies and bearing gifts such as complimentary bottles of water and their unique brand of hospitality. This is the signature Newfoundlander approach to a gathering. Timing is subject to the weather and once the game is on, everyone, and I mean everyone, gets in on it. It is this spontaneity and all or nothing attitude that makes a Newfoundland party so special.

Shouting with a friendly enthusiastic tone, we heard:

> Organizer #1: Where's your captain now, ladies, we best get this ship out to sea.

As she and Mary stood speaking, our opposition arrived and, as if they owned the place, immediately took to the field for a warmup. The Rainbows stood watching, sizing them up.

> Tannis: Big fuckin' mothers, aren't they?
> Susan: Yeah, I hope I don't get caught under one of them.
> Kathy: Me too, the only part of you that would survive would be your fingernails.
> Angie: We'll beat 'em with our speed, ooohh, I can't wait to get out there. I bet they hit nothing but flies.

I too was looking forward to playing my game in Canada's most easterly province. I had played ball from coast to coast, and from south to north. Burnaby B.C. to Mount Pearl, Newfoundland. Calgary, Saskatoon, and Grand-Mere, Quebec, and many of our wonderful, quirky small towns in between. I had even played ball as a kid in Ross River, Yukon, which is 410 kilometres north of Whitehorse, the capital of that territory, and Whitehorse is already north enough for dog mushing and gold panning.

I had played ball all across my country, against some of Canada's most enthusiastic and talented recreational athletes. I had been part of a throng of ball players that responded to SPN's challenge to play our game together at the highest possible level of amateur, recreational sport. Although playing a sport for nothing more than the pleasure of it can result in knee and shoulder replacements, it can also result in great memories and friendships. I had been given an abundance of both.

As I swung a bat and watched our opposition on the diamond, I sensed the kind of relief one gets when a long run at something is coming to an end. In those final days or hours, we get sentimental and talk about the good old days as if they were nothing but tulips and roses. Like the talk at a retirement party, when everyone is telling the retiree how much she will be missed and how going outside in a snowstorm to have a smoke will just never be the same. And the retiree, who had suffered in silence for the last twenty years because she hated her windowless office and never got to take customers out for lunch, is thinking, maybe she shouldn't go quite yet. Who will she have a smoke and gossip with now? Who's going to listen to her complain about her husband on Monday mornings? Who's going to bring her a double double and her favourite doughnut on her birthday?

Mary was back, an official scorebook in her hand.

Mary: Looks like there won't be any special rules for warmup. Let's go everybody, grab your mitts and a ball, and warm up. And hustle, we've only got ten minutes!

While we played our game the entire ball park was transformed from what had at first appeared to be a deserted, litter strewn backwater to a full-on east coast fling. Barbeques appeared and burgers were sizzling, cold cans of Canadians and Coors Light glittered under the ice inside huge metal tubs and Newfoundlanders of every age and size were selling them from the concession stand while music blared from a ghetto blaster.

In Calgary, public events involving barbeques, beef and beer are planned months in advance and executed by an organizing committee and sub-committees that report weekly to the Chair of the Organizing Committee, and involve Third Party Quality

Control, Health and Safety inspections, and Sponsorships dutifully flaunted with ten foot long banners worth $1000 each. For entertainment, there is usually a platinum award winning country and western band from Nashville, and an appearance by at least one high profile politician. And of course a couple of oil barons. And everyone is dressed really, really, well. These parties go off without a hitch and are attended by hundreds of people who are either employees of or wannabe employees of an oil baron, along with unlimited numbers of friends and relatives. Calgary is so famous for these slick events that when the local chapter of Slo-Pitch National hosted the Nationals, they didn't host a party because, I suspect, they didn't have the budget needed for one that would measure up to the Calgary standard.

The Newfoundland approach to hosting a national competition was, let's say, enlightening. Who knew that with nothing more than a few decrepit barbecues and a ghetto blaster, an unlimited supply of at- cost ice cold beers, and not a single oil baron within 100 leagues, people could have so much fun? In fact, we had a whale of a good time. And it was just the opening day.

The Rainbows won that first game and a few more, but our greatest victory was keeping pace with the party boat, which clipped along non-stop from point to point, stopping only to refill the beer bucket, which was almost, but not quite, bottomless. When the Rainbows did finally hit the bottom, we had to switch to screech and kiss a cod. This classic Newfoundland cultural rite took place at an old clapboard hall that looked like it may have been the centre of the Mount Pearl and St. John's community since the beginning of time. Big enough to house the entire population of the community, hundreds of ball players, a live local band and a gigantic wooden oar, the hall was the scene of not only Janet's indiscretion with a dead fish but also the beginning of Angie's downfall.

The famous Newfoundland hospitality was in full swing, a better party could not have been found anywhere in Mount

Pearl that night, because all the residents of the town were there, many of them wearing mustard yellow rubber rain slicks in case a nor'wester blew in. Jigs and reels and ballads performed by men in such outfits are captivating, sure, but even more so when accompanied by screech and fried and battered samplings from the sea. Served by the fine community minded ladies and gentlemen of Mount Pearl, the generosity of those Atlantic waters and its people proved fathomless, as did Angie's capacity for consumption. Mostly of the liquid offerings, that is.

For the record, Angie flexed her Molson muscle all night not only to show the locals that an Albertan could keep up, but also to expend a surplus of self-satisfaction she had acquired after a day of ball during which she played at her peak. In particular, she ran the bases well. So well did Angie run the bases she felt genuine pain each time another Rainbow transgressed the standard she had set. So great was her pain she yelled, shouted, and even swore at any Rainbow that transgressed her base running expectations, which, Angie discovered the next day, were severely deficient in several qualities. Particularly humility and prescience.

The rest of the Rainbows partook of the Saturday night festivities with abandon until Janet did finally kiss the cod. At that point it became evident that the party was going to go on without us. It was Saturday night, after all, the biggest night of the week for the locals who did not, like the Rainbows, have to play ball the next morning. While the bulk of the team headed for the hotel, there were a few who did not. These happened to be Rainbows who held key positions. You know who they are, but for clarity, here are the names: Angie, Kathy, Sherry. These three, being highly competitive, were not about to be outdone by the locals and therefore, came to Sunday's game in severe distress.

This distress led to Angie's comeuppance:

The Rainbows are on the bats. Kathy's on first and Angie, whose bleary bloodshot eyes are, on the colour wheel, outperforming her blue eyeshadow, is up. Our opponents are a gang of ball busters but despite their hitting power, we're hanging on due to our nimble defence and tenacious base hits which keep the score tight. The pitcher is giving Angie nothing to work with so finally she takes a pitch and hits a high fly. She drops the bat and runs. Kathy had taken the standard four steps away from the base and is waiting to see if the fielder will catch the fly. The ball takes one of those leisurely rides up and then dangles in the sky a moment, before beginning its descent. As if someone has hit the pause button on a remote control, fielders, basewomen, and the one runner, Kathy, who must tag up if the ball is caught, all hold their positions until the outcome of the fly ball is known.

Angie, however, tears up the baseline, rounds first and heads for second, passing Kathy who is still waiting to see if she will need to tag up.

Debbie:	No Angie no! Go back to first!
Janet:	Back to first Angie to first…
Mary:	Angie! Go, to, first!

Perhaps it's the pickle juice still lingering in her veins. Perhaps it's her unassailable belief in her base running prowess. Something, in any case, prevents her from comprehending the shouted instructions of the base coach and the back-up shouts of the very Rainbows she had lambasted the day before, and so, she finishes her astonishing run to second base and proceeds to jump up and down, thoroughly satisfied with herself. Until she sees Kathy walking off the field toward the Rainbow bench, and the facts begin to penetrate her foggy mind.

Mary:	Come in Ang! You're out!

She returns to the dugout, befuddled, bewildered, and in need of a security guard to help her maneuver past the irate Rainbows she had chastened the day before.

THE RAINBOWS WHO IN 2001 WERE SNEAKING PEAKS OVER THE cliff edge of fifty didn't notice the signs that said, 'peak performance requires 8 hours of sleep per night, oatmeal and fruit for breakfast, lean proteins and plenty of vegetables at lunch and dinner, and a limit of one beer per day'.

However, that day, a number of Rainbows did take an afternoon nap. Somewhere there is a photograph of limp, Kelly green clad bodies splayed upon the scanty grass that grows on the Rock.

Part 2

AFTER THE TOURNAMENT, THE RAINBOWS TOURED THE MARITIMES. We saw the Bluenose and Peggy's Cove, we ate Digby scallops, drank Alexander Keith's in the brewery district of Halifax, got chased out of the Bay of Fundy by the tide. We crossed the brand new Confederation Bridge and while some of us played golf, others walked the red sandy beaches of PEI and swam in the warm waters of the Northumberland Strait, climbed over sand dunes, and saw where all those McCain potatoes are grown and possibly got our hands caught in a lobster trap. We drove the entirety of the Cape Breton coast along Cabot Trail, passing through Magee, the home of the Rankins who, unfortunately, were not home, and stayed in towns with names I still cannot pronounce. Like Antigonish. Oh it looks easy enough, but after hundreds of attempts, I could not get a single local to approve my pronunciation. I might get it once, but on my second try their faces would fall. No one but maritimers can talk like a maritimer.

But before leaving Newfoundland to do all that, we went to Cape Spear to stand on the most easterly point of the North American continent. Be careful if you do this, there is a risk of gale force winds blasting you off the rock and tossing you into St. John's harbour. Just in case, consider visiting Cape Spear in a wetsuit. Finally, to cap off our tour of the Rock, we spent a night on St. John's famous George Street.

George Street is filled with bars and pubs each with its own family band playing inside. Patrons can stroll, and later stumble up and down the cobblestoned street, popping in and out of the pubs according to their whim. If they feel a little nippy, a hot dog vendor is there ready and waiting, and so are the police, who, on the warm summer night we visited, maintained a notable and friendly presence. Since there was no hint of conflict, it was hard to imagine why there were so many of them. Perhaps the officers had brothers or cousins or aunties playing in the many bands and they wanted to have a listen. The locals and tourists mingled and danced Irish jigs with nothing but sheer drunken joy, not a single sign of trouble. Not even when Kerry's husband, Jack, (of Jack and the Cracks fame), was being fawned over by a bevy of local women who took a real shine to his chubby baby face and twinkling blue eyes.

They said he looked just like a local b'y with those cheeks and eyes. He could have been one of their brothers, they said, except, since he wasn't, they didn't mind giving him a little peck on the cheek, and wouldn't it be so charming just to sit on his cozy lap, he was such a sweetheart, just for a little cuddle? They just dies for him, they said, and wanted to know who knit him, he was just so darling, and wasn't his wife a sweetie too, not to be getting' all contrary as the b'y was being pawed over and sat upon. Jack himself, being a well-raised prairie farm boy, was too polite to object. No other Husband had been singled out by the local ladies. The smile on Jack's face was as jolly as Santa's at the company's adult only Christmas party. For one night, he was treated as a genuine stud muffin.

Not wanting to spoil Jack's fun, Kerry sipped her shandy and along with the rest of the Rainbows and Rainbow Husbands, sat back and enjoyed the entertainment. After all that, Jack was mighty quiet. I suspect he was wondering if he had been misplaced at birth, or if he should take up farming down east. Although there's little in the way of farming in Newfoundland, he could maybe pick up a potato farm over the water and visit the Rock on weekends.

Kerry probably would have let him try it out, knowing he'd come hightailing it back home when he realized all those maritimers eat is fish and chips and lobster sandwiches.

It was in the same pub where Jack's picture is now displayed that I discovered my feet were born preprogrammed to take control of my body the moment they heard the music of the Irish. The fiddle bows of the band in that pub were crisscrossing through the air like clippers in a stormy sea, and the shoes of dozens of dancers were pounding the wood floor like it was the door to eternity. Mesmerized by the sounds, I followed my feet to the dance floor and felt the thunder, the fire, the freedom, the home, and the heart of the River Dance style songs coursing through my flesh and bones. Feet pounding, heels turning, soul sailing, I danced through the heat of that summer night on George Street until all I had to give to that celebration of life had been given.

The whole world should go to George Street on a summer Saturday night. There is something in that Irish music that demands its listeners turn over the controls and allow themselves to be taken away to a place where pure raw life explodes in every wild note.

CHAPTER 38

THAT MARITIME CANADA HIGH THAT THE RAINBOWS CAME HOME on the summer of 2001, and the Rainbows slo-pitch odyssey, were both gently approaching a soft landing at home plate when New York's twin towers were brought down, and the lives of us all came, for a moment, to a crashing halt. That dreadful day the world discovered Newfoundlanders' genuine hospitality and *heart*. Sadly, this came with the realization that terrorism was on the rise and could happen anywhere.

While I sat on my living room sofa and watched CNN run the horror over and over and over, I felt within me an acute awareness of the tenuous nature of our lives, both physical and conceptual.

This belief we had in a free and peaceful world that guaranteed us long and prosperous lives was challenged on North American soil in a way no one of my generation had ever before seen or imagined. I remember, who of us will ever forget, the moment, the place, the details of that day—9/11, 2001.

Yet. Like millions of other ball players and sports fans, the heart of the Rainbows continues to beat strong and sure. After twenty years of pumping blood through our collective aorta, when the girls get together all the arteries are still wide open and connect so smoothly it's as if there are invisible little scrubbers keeping the rust off. The Rainbows would never have thought of themselves as an experiment, a microcosm of our era – a blend of hilariously diverse individuals each with a bat hitting freedom and friendship balls out of the park. But that is what we were and that is what we did and man oh man, did we ever do it right.

In that last year, 2001, at the Okotoks Ladies Slo-pitch Association AGM, the Rainbows received a standing ovation from the members of the association. Most members of the league teams had come for the meeting and to say goodbye to the Rainbows. The President of the association gave a speech, a tribute, to our team. Her words were gracious and generous and drew warm applause.

The Rainbows were flabbergasted. We had no idea, no expectation, that such a tribute would be bestowed on us at the meeting. We were just there together to raise a glass and say goodbye to the league and to each other. 'It's been a great ride girls, it's been a great ride'.

Kathy, naturally, was a little suspicious.

Kathy: Are they really applauding because we held it together for 20 straight years, or because they're so happy to see us go?

We laughed. We were the nemesis of many of the league's teams, after all. But this wasn't because rivals like the Mavericks and Kinfolk didn't try their damnedest to beat us and they occasionally did, or that the Fountain Tire Flyers didn't have plenty of talent on their team. It was because we played with such a sense of abandon, such a sense of glee, and of freedom. We played, and we accepted each other as teammates, within that field of grace. Nothing short of the ending of the world as we know it can overcome grace.

LIKE THE BURST OF SPEED OF A YOUNGER RAINBOW CHASING A home run, time took off when the team retired. While my old teammates were perfecting their golf and curling games, I retired from team sports and focused on sharpening my political skills at the MD of Foothills and finishing that tiresome university degree.

Meanwhile, my children were collectively flying the coop post high school or university graduation.

Having your children fly the coop is a shocking experience that I would like to have shared with the Rainbows. I could have used their practical feedback, which I'm sure would have helped me put things into perspective. I imagine it like this:

Me:	When Ben took his last bag out the door and left the house I bawled worse than a calf looking for its mom.
Debbie:	What were you crying for? Didn't he just get his own place in Calgary?
Me:	Yeah but he's all grown up, all of them have grown up!
Kathy:	Isn't that supposed to be a good thing?
Karen:	You bet your booties that's a good thing.
Sherry:	If it's that bad you can always have another one like I did.
Angie:	Hahaha, I can just hear Rob now if I told him I wanted to have a baby, he'd quit sleeping with me but can you imagine having another baby oh my god I'd have to hire one of those ninnies I don't think I'd even be able to anyway we're too old now aren't we....?
Kathy:	Oh for crying out loud Angie you wouldn't have to hire a ninny *you're* a ninny....

Since I still could not produce a single coherent piece of writing, I bumbled and stumbled through the next years, looking, looking, looking, for the right path.

I went down numerous dead ends. Such as stints as, (in no particular order) a cheese monger, an electric gate designer, a real estate salesperson, and a quasi-political scientist. There were investigative based forays into provincial and federal politics that took me to: local riding meetings where the real strings are pulled; the inside, and I mean the very guts, of the voting crisis when Stockwell Day and Preston Manning had their leadership contest; the Bay Street Stock Exchange, by invitation, for the inaugural gathering of keeners behind the Manning Centre for Building Democracy, which, thankfully, caused me to close the book on further efforts in the political 'hypocrisydome'.

Eventually I realized I was going nowhere so I went to my doctor who sent me to a therapist who in less than half an hour helped me pull the truth up out of my soul: I needed to go away for a long time and write a book that was screaming to come out but refused to do so until I took myself away from Husband and home.

I went to Australia, wrote my first book, worked out some problems, and came home. When I next saw my old teammates, they came to my new house where I was living alone and continuing to write.

Susan:	So, you wrote a book! What's it about?
Me:	It's about a white girl who moves to an indigenous community in the Yukon.
Susan:	Neat! Is it a true story?
Me:	Yes and no – it's based on my experience but it's fiction.
Angie:	I haven't read a book in so long. When I try I always fall asleep but I'll read yours Michele that's for sure.
Sonny:	That's pretty cool Michele, is it hard to write a book?
Me:	Yes.

When the girls left I noticed my house felt more complete. I poured myself a glass of wine, they had all insisted on just having coffee, and gave a toast to my old team, the Rainbows.

CHAPTER 39

I THINK SHERRY MUST HAVE LOVED THE OLD TROOPER SONG, "We're Here for a Good Time, Not a Long Time". She lived that song and never talked about her illness. When she died in 2013, for the memorial service her family asked the Rainbows to form a symbolic passageway for them as they carried Sherry out of the hall. As I stood with my old teammates I looked around at the variety of greens we had chosen to wear. We had considered wearing our uniforms but decided Sherry would have scoffed at the idea had she been going to one of our funerals.

Catching up with the girls over a glass of wine later, I heard details of all the golfing and curling and grandkids of the retired ones, and the work and growing families of the younger ones. Although I always had an idea what everyone was up to, thanks to Debbie, who keeps the circle intact through email, it was good to hear all the stories. And it felt good to be with them, even though it was for Sherry's funeral, the first funeral.

Sooner or later, it will be my turn, I thought. And these old friends, those who have not gone before me, will come to my service. I took comfort in that thought. Maybe one or two might speak to my kids, tell them a story or two, say how much fun we had together. Maybe give away some of my secrets. Ruth would have done that for sure, but we lost her in 2016. The Rainbows put together a lunch for Ruth's service and it felt right to honour her in that way. She was our number one fan.

Husbands also go, as Angie's did in 2017. Many Rainbows were there to support her at the service. What more can we ask of life than to belong, always, to a family, to a circle of friends, to a tribe, or team? We may source our own food, shelter, and clothing independently but who needs any of that if we can't share it, offer it, laugh at it, loan it or like it? Today or yesterday, tomorrow or next year, my life has meaning because, even way out here in right field, I have lifelines to friends, family, old teammates. When I'm with them, I feel that belonging, and gratitude that I hold within me these memories and the knowledge I am a part of this circle of friends, and always will be.

EPILOGUE

A PHONE CALL FROM JOSH:

Josh:	Hey, you busy this afternoon?
Me:	Not necessarily. What's up?
Josh:	I've got a mixed slo-pitch game today. We need another girl. You in?
Me:	Hehehehe, that might not be such a good idea. I haven't played since the Rainbows retired.
Josh:	Once a ball player, always a ball player. The game's at 2:00 PM. Be there.

None of my children knew the secret of my throwing problem. Until their father and I divorced, I had managed to keep them in the dark about most of my weaknesses and failings, so they mostly believed I was a star ball player and all-rounder in matters of life and living.

Since I hadn't played for close to fifteen years, I didn't know if my psychogenic hypochondria was gone or just waiting in a dark corner to be reactivated. Of course, the balls used in the game were still oversized, so there would be that. But as a Rainbow I had enjoyed ball seasons during which I threw the ball well enough, and so, had never come to a firm conclusion as to what was wrong with me all those years.

Should I take the chance? I didn't want Josh thinking of me as a used up ball player. Especially since the pitcher on his regular men's team was at least fifteen years older than I. Josh was almost thirty.

I called him back.

Me: Okay, I'll come out but I should just play catcher. My arm won't be in any kind of shape for much else.
Josh: We'll see.

I arrived at the diamond and sized up the team, which consisted of a mix of young guys and a few girls who were good sports, making their boyfriends happy by playing with them so they could impress their girlfriends with their physical prowess.

I warmed up with Josh and just like the old days, the ball felt like a new age watermelon in my hand.

Josh: Looks like the team needs someone to take first. You good with that?
Me: Sure, that'll work.

The trouble with playing first base is there's no time to reflect on things like there is in right field. Not only is the first base person just 30 feet from the batter and therefore vulnerable to cracked jaws, she also receives throws from all other players when trying to put the batter out on the run to first. It can be fatal to let your mind wander with thoughts of past sports victories, of past athletic ability, or of all the hours spent rolling and tossing balls with the child who is now hucking a ball the distance of the entire field and infield straight into home plate and putting out the runner who was ripping up the dirt at a decent pace considering it was a Sunday and he was straight off an all-nighter.

Playing a sport with my adult children brings me a kind of satisfaction that no other activity with them delivers. There is something deep in a sporting mother's soul that is only touched when she sees and engages with her adult child competently throwing, batting, shooting, spiking, driving, bouncing, kicking, a ball. Knowing that in their muscles live memories of those first years, sitting on their diaper clad bottoms, legs spread wide and pudgy hands out, waiting to reach for the big blue plastic ball rolling down the hallway toward them. Knowing their strong legs got started out in the yard chasing after and trying, trying, trying, to kick that same ball and the memory in their heart muscle when they did kick it, and scored on Mommy.

Knowing that in their soul are freefalling sun-soaked images of chasing after dreams.

Fortunately, there were no serious incidents. I acquitted myself with enough catches and outs on first to have added value, and, although I didn't get any nice hard line drives up the middle, I didn't strike out either. My son could hold his head up. He would not have to apologize for suggesting his mother fill in. I considered this a success, but I did not feel the need to play again.

That was my last slo-pitch game.

Now, I play singles tennis. It's easier on my psyches and if I make a bad play I let no one down but myself. My kids play with me once in a while, when they're not playing basketball, or football, or volleyball, or golfing. I still refuse to take up golf. My knees are still good, I think it's the hiking. I gave my little grandsons each a tennis racquet, maybe they'll take a shine to the game, but I am also looking forward to throwing a few softballs with them when they're old enough.

The view from right field these days is bigger than ever. Too enormous for words.

The Rainbows, Mount Pearl, Newfoundland, 2001, Author is right side, second from front

ABOUT THE AUTHOR

MICHELE MOORE VELDHOEN SPENT MUCH OF HER CHILDHOOD IN out of the way BC towns. In 1978, while still in high school, she moved to Calgary, Alberta, where she continues to reside. After years of working in a family business, studying, raising her children, and taking exploratory trips down many different paths, she finally became a passionate teacher of English to speakers of other languages, and began to realize her most enduring dream, to be a writer. *A View From Right Field* is not her first project, but it is the first to be published.

www.ingramcontent.com/pod-product-compliance
Lightning Source LLC
Chambersburg PA
CBHW020903080526
44589CB00011B/422